Microsoft System Center PowerShell Essentials

Efficiently administer, automate, and manage System Center environments using Windows PowerShell

Guruprasad HP

Harshul Patel

PUBLISHING

BIRMINGHAM - MUMBAI

Microsoft System Center PowerShell Essentials

First published: April 2015

Production reference: 1240415

Published by Packt Publishing Ltd.
Livery Place
35 Livery Street
Birmingham B3 2PB, UK.

ISBN 978-1-78439-714-2

www.packtpub.com

Credits

Authors
Guruprasad HP
Harshul Patel

Reviewers
Lee Boon Cheng
Richard Gibson
Keith Lindsay
Ashley Poole

Commissioning Editor
Dipika Gaonkar

Acquisition Editor
Sonali Vernekar

Content Development Editor
Rahul Nair

Technical Editors
Mrunmayee Patil
Manal Pednekar

Copy Editors
Sonia Michelle Cheema
Neha Vyas

Project Coordinator
Suzanne Coutinho

Proofreaders
Safis Editing
Paul Hindle

Indexer
Mariammal Chettiyar

Production Coordinator
Arvindkumar Gupta

Cover Work
Arvindkumar Gupta

About the Authors

Guruprasad HP is a technical practitioner and consultant. His technical areas of interest include System Center Configuration Manager, System Center Operation Manager, and automation using PowerShell scripting. He works with Microsoft and is a Microsoft Certified Technology Specialist in SCCM and SCOM.

He has a lot of experience in creating automation frameworks for various activities in SCCM, SCOM, and custom reporting by extending the SCCM inventory. He also has good knowledge of all Microsoft technologies.

Currently, Guruprasad is working with Microsoft as a consultant and is involved in various projects with different Microsoft technologies.

I would like to thank all my well-wishers who identified my skills and encouraged and guided me whenever required. I will take this opportunity to thank my mother for being the backbone of my life.

I would also like to thank my friend Kishora V, who stood with me morally and without whom I would not have achieved many things in my life. It's a great pleasure to work with my friend and the coauthor of this book, Harshul, who always keeps my technical spirits up with new information.

I would also like to thank each and every person who directly or indirectly supported me in learning and practicing various technologies.

Harshul Patel is a technology enthusiast from India; he is thoroughly knowledgeable in virtualization and cloud computing techniques. He works for Microsoft. Harshul holds multiple Microsoft certifications, including Microsoft Certified Solutions Associate (Windows Server 2012 and Windows 8) and Microsoft Certified Solutions Expert (private cloud). Additionally, he holds a number of non-Microsoft certifications, such as Citrix Certified Administrator (XenApp 6.5, XenDesktop 5.6, and XenServer 6.0) and Citrix Certified Advanced Administrator (XenApp 6.5). He has also recently achieved an ITIL certification.

Harshul was one of the early Indian adopters of Windows PowerShell. He frequently lectures on Windows PowerShell in user group gatherings and delivers training (mostly on PowerShell) across various organizations. He is also a proud recipient of multiple faculty awards and has received an innovation award from his employer. He is a core member of the PowerShell Bangalore User Group (http://powershellgroup.org/bangalore.india) and a member of the New Delhi PowerShell User Group (http://powershellgroup.org/NewDelhi). He can be contacted at http://harshulpatel.com/.

Harshul authored a book in 2013 named *Instant Windows PowerShell Guide, Packt Publishing* (https://www.packtpub.com/application-development/instant-windows-powershell-guide-instant).

I would like to thank all those who have encouraged me all the time and made me feel that I have the potential to do whatever I want. I am very thankful to my family members and especially to my friends, for helping me to get things done. Without learning from these people, there would be no chance that I would be doing what I do today, and it is because of them and others, whom I may not have listed here, that I feel compelled to pass my knowledge on to those willing to learn.

I would especially like to thank Guruprasad HP (the coauthor of this book) for his flawless support in drafting this book's chapters at short notice. I would like to thank the Indian PowerShell community, including MVPs Ravikanth Chaganti, Aman Dhally, and Deepak Dhami, for their contribution and inspiration.

Finally, many thanks to the Almighty for making this possible.

About the Reviewers

Lee Boon Cheng is a computer engineering graduate from Nanyang Technological University of Singapore. He is currently working as a SharePoint solution architect in a commodity trading company in Singapore.

He has worked on and led multiple Microsoft SharePoint 2010/2013 projects for Singapore clients ranging from schools to corporations to government departments. He has primarily focused on the SharePoint Content Management System, workflow and SharePoint installation, and configuration and deployment using PowerShell.

> I would like to thank my wife, Kathryn Saw, for always being supportive of what I do.

Richard Gibson lives in London and has worked as a .NET developer for 8 years. His work has taken him into the world of DevOps, and PowerShell has become a necessary skill for the automation of everyday tasks.

He currently works for ASOS.com as a senior developer, spending most of his PowerShell time automating TeamCity to provide continuous deployment for the business. Richard blogs on various issues related to .NET and PowerShell at http://richiban.uk/.

Keith Lindsay graduated from Sacred Heart University with honors and spent nearly a decade as a software engineer. After deciding that he wanted to explore a new path, he moved into the field of product management for Citrix ShareFile, where he uses his technical skills to help improve and promote the API and SDKs. He is a big proponent of PowerShell and has helped his company to develop a PowerShell SDK for file sharing. You can read more about using PowerShell for file sharing on his blog at `http://blogs.citrix.com/author/keithl1/`.

I would like to especially thank Peter Schulz for mentoring me in the ways of PowerShell.

Ashley Poole is a highly motivated software support analyst with over 6 years of professional experience in the field of IT. Normally, you can find him exploring topics such as Microsoft SQL Server, C#, PowerShell, and Dev Ops.

More recently, he can also be found exploring software development technologies and practices, as he begins his journey into the world of software development.

Ashley can also be found blogging on various IT and software topics on his website, `www.ashleypoole.co.uk`, tweeting as `@AshleyPooleUK`, or sharing open source projects and scripts for the community at `https://github.com/AshleyPoole`.

www.PacktPub.com

Support files, eBooks, discount offers, and more

For support files and downloads related to your book, please visit www.PacktPub.com.

Did you know that Packt offers eBook versions of every book published, with PDF and ePub files available? You can upgrade to the eBook version at www.PacktPub.com and as a print book customer, you are entitled to a discount on the eBook copy. Get in touch with us at service@packtpub.com for more details.

At www.PacktPub.com, you can also read a collection of free technical articles, sign up for a range of free newsletters and receive exclusive discounts and offers on Packt books and eBooks.

https://www2.packtpub.com/books/subscription/packtlib

Do you need instant solutions to your IT questions? PacktLib is Packt's online digital book library. Here, you can search, access, and read Packt's entire library of books.

Why subscribe?

- Fully searchable across every book published by Packt
- Copy and paste, print, and bookmark content
- On demand and accessible via a web browser

Free access for Packt account holders

If you have an account with Packt at www.PacktPub.com, you can use this to access PacktLib today and view 9 entirely free books. Simply use your login credentials for immediate access.

Instant updates on new Packt books

Get notified! Find out when new books are published by following @PacktEnterprise on Twitter or the *Packt Enterprise* Facebook page.

Table of Contents

Preface

Microsoft System Center PowerShell Essentials mainly focuses on efficiently administering, automating, and managing System Center environments using Windows PowerShell. This book will help you to create powerful automation scripts for System Center products using PowerShell; PowerShell techniques efficiently handle SCCM, SCOM, and SCSM with real-time examples and sample codes. It is a step-by-step guide with practical examples and best practices that teaches you how to effectively use PowerShell in a System Center environment.

Microsoft PowerShell as a scripting language has been growing strongly over the last couple of years. It has given administrators and IT professionals much more control over managing and implementing tasks within System Center environments. It provides vast support for a wide range of vendor products and provides a standardized platform for automation and administration. System Center facilitates the configuration, monitoring, and management of the components of private cloud. It covers products such as SCCM, SCOM, SCSM, SCVMM, and so on.

Starting with an introduction to PowerShell, this quick reference guide will enable you to get the most out of the latest Microsoft PowerShell techniques to manage System Center products. You will get acquainted with the enhancements in the latest version of System Center automation through real-time examples.

By the end of this book, you will have the confidence to create a variety of PowerShell scripts and efficiently administer and maintain your System Center environment with PowerShell.

What this book covers

Chapter 1, Setting up the Environment to Use PowerShell, gives you an idea about the purpose of this book, and how to set up the environment with required modules for three products, SCCM, SCOM, and SCSM.

Chapter 2, Administration of Configuration Manager through PowerShell, focuses on administration activities for Configuration Manager, such as inventory, discovery, alert management, and so on.

Chapter 3, Scenario-based Scripting for SCCM Administration, gives you an insight into SCCM real-time applications by giving various scenarios, which are explained with the help of the required code blocks.

Chapter 4, Administration of Operations Manager through PowerShell, focuses on administration activities for Operations Manager, such as monitoring, authoring, basic administration, and so on.

Chapter 5, Scenario-based Scripting for SCOM Administration, gives you an insight into SCOM real-time applications by providing various scenarios, which are explained with the help of the required code blocks.

Chapter 6, Administration of Service Manager through PowerShell, focuses on the administration activities of Service Manager, such as the use of SMlets, incident reporting, managing service requests, and so on.

Chapter 7, Scenario-based Scripting for SCSM Administration, gives you more insight into SCSM real-time applications by providing various scenarios, which are explained with the help of the required code blocks.

Chapter 8, Best Practices, focuses on real-time applications, which can be used to derive best practices for these three products.

What you need for this book

You need to have these products to take full advantage of this book:

- Windows PowerShell (v2.0 or higher)
- System Center Configuration Manager (2007 or higher)
- System Center Operational Manager (2010 or higher)
- System Center Service Manager (2010 or higher)

Who this book is for

If you are a Microsoft System Center administrator who manages System Center environments and utilizes the console for management, then this book is ideal for you. This book is also for System Center users who now want to learn how to manage systems using PowerShell.

Conventions

In this book, you will find a number of text styles that distinguish between different kinds of information. Here are some examples of these styles and an explanation of their meaning.

Code words in text, database table names, folder names, filenames, file extensions, pathnames, dummy URLs, user input, and Twitter handles are shown as follows: "For example, we will refer to the parent installation folder as C:\Program Files(x86)."

A block of code is set as follows:

```
$UserRoleArgs = @{
   UserRoleType = "ReadOnlyOperator"
   DisplayName = "restricted role"
   Queue = @()
   Group = @()
   Task = @()
   User = "PSLAB\SCSMUser01"
   }
New-SCSMUserRole @UserRoleArgs
```

Any command-line input or output is written as follows:

```
PS C :\> cd "C:\Program Files(x86)\Microsoft Configuration Manager\
AdminConsole\bin"
```

New terms and **important words** are shown in bold. Words that you see on the screen, for example, in menus or dialog boxes, appear in the text like this: "In the **Service Manager** console, click on **Administration**."

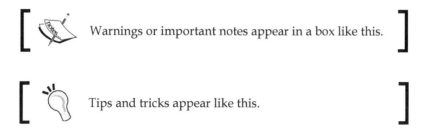

Warnings or important notes appear in a box like this.

Tips and tricks appear like this.

Reader feedback

Feedback from our readers is always welcome. Let us know what you think about this book—what you liked or disliked. Reader feedback is important for us as it helps us develop titles that you will really get the most out of.

To send us general feedback, simply e-mail `feedback@packtpub.com`, and mention the book's title in the subject of your message.

If there is a topic that you have expertise in and you are interested in either writing or contributing to a book, see our author guide at `www.packtpub.com/authors`.

Customer support

Now that you are the proud owner of a Packt book, we have a number of things to help you to get the most from your purchase.

Downloading the example code

You can download the example code files from your account at `http://www.packtpub.com` for all the Packt Publishing books you have purchased. If you purchased this book elsewhere, you can visit `http://www.packtpub.com/support` and register to have the files e-mailed directly to you.

Errata

Although we have taken every care to ensure the accuracy of our content, mistakes do happen. If you find a mistake in one of our books—maybe a mistake in the text or the code—we would be grateful if you could report this to us. By doing so, you can save other readers from frustration and help us improve subsequent versions of this book. If you find any errata, please report them by visiting `http://www.packtpub.com/submit-errata`, selecting your book, clicking on the **Errata Submission Form** link, and entering the details of your errata. Once your errata are verified, your submission will be accepted and the errata will be uploaded to our website or added to any list of existing errata under the Errata section of that title.

To view the previously submitted errata, go to `https://www.packtpub.com/books/content/support` and enter the name of the book in the search field. The required information will appear under the **Errata** section.

Piracy

Piracy of copyrighted material on the Internet is an ongoing problem across all media. At Packt, we take the protection of our copyright and licenses very seriously. If you come across any illegal copies of our works in any form on the Internet, please provide us with the location address or website name immediately so that we can pursue a remedy.

Please contact us at `copyright@packtpub.com` with a link to the suspected pirated material.

We appreciate your help in protecting our authors and our ability to bring you valuable content.

Questions

If you have a problem with any aspect of this book, you can contact us at `questions@packtpub.com`, and we will do our best to address the problem.

1
Setting up the Environment to Use PowerShell

Welcome! In this introductory chapter, we will throw some light on how the idea for this book came in to our minds. Here, we will cover topics that can help users perform various routine tasks in the System Center environment by using legacy consoles. A decade back, an administrator had to go with legacy Microsoft Management Consoles, broadly known as MMC, for most of the Microsoft products. Now, with the changes in the architecture of the Microsoft products and the birth of automation engines such as Windows PowerShell, automation has become easy; however, many of us are not fully aware of it. Let's start with setting up the environment.

In this chapter, we will cover:

- The purpose of this book
- The target audience
- Why use PowerShell?
- PowerShell version references
- Setting up the System Center Configuration Manager environment
- Setting up the System Center Operations Manager environment
- Setting up the System Center Service Manager environment

The purpose of this book

This book will help you to achieve the idea of automation, especially in the System Center environment using Windows PowerShell. The purpose of this book is to provide you with an insight of various PowerShell techniques that can be applied to the following three System Center products:

- **System Center Configuration Manager (SCCM)**
- **System Center Operations Manager (SCOM)**
- **System Center Service Manager (SCSM)**

We will also highlight how to use the various PowerShell cmdlets available with these three product SDKs, along with their key tips and tricks. All guidance and assistance will be provided to you on a high-level basis. Further exploration and hands-on experience for these three products is required, so that you gain the most out of this book.

The target audience

This book is aimed mainly at IT professionals who maintain or perform routine activities in the System Center environment focusing on SCCM, SCOM, and SCSM products. This book will be very useful for people who seek out-of-the-box automation for their System Center infrastructure, using Windows PowerShell. You will find real time use of Windows PowerShell with these System Center products.

Why use PowerShell?

In the last few years, the scripting world has witnessed a number of changes. We can hardly recall the time when people used ancient mainframe machines with green-colored text and dark, black-screen backgrounds. Times have changed and we are living in a world where technological adoption is quicker than ever.

Nowadays, an ample number of scripting languages exist, which fulfill the needs of an administrator. One of the questions that arise in one's mind is: why should we go with Windows PowerShell? There are reasons why we prefer Windows PowerShell over other scripting languages. To answer the preceding question precisely, we would rather put a counter question in front of you: give us a valid reason why we shouldn't go with Windows PowerShell.

There are other examples of strong scripting languages, such as VBScript, Ruby, Python, Perl, and so on, and administrators have adopted them too. VBScript became popular because of the automation of routine, local administrator tasks, but the code was a bit complex and hard to understand for novice users. Looking at Windows PowerShell, we feel that the Microsoft team has worked hard to give us a powerful, interactive scripting shell with an object-driven approach.

The important and exciting thing about this language is that it's a spitted object-based output, which can be reused easily. It has **pipeline** and **PSRemoting** as its crucial features, which put this language as the first priority while comparing it with other scripting languages. Moreover, by following the **Common Engineering Criteria (CEC)**, Microsoft has decided that all future Microsoft products will come with extensive Windows PowerShell support. This is also a good reason to learn and choose Windows PowerShell. Additionally, PowerShell can be leveraged to use the massive .Net Framework class functionality with most of the Microsoft products. We can also achieve inventory and reporting by efficiently using the WMI functionality that lies within PowerShell. A few Microsoft products support extensive functionality when used with PowerShell; the best example is Exchange Server.

PowerShell version references

In this section, we shall talk about the various versions of Windows PowerShell that are available and we will share a few notes on the latest versions v3.0 and v4.0, along with their preinstallation requirements and dependencies.

So far, we have had four stable versions available for Windows PowerShell. Windows PowerShell v1.0 was an extension of Command Prompt with a limited number of cmdlets. In the second version, the team introduced pipeline and PSRemoting concepts, which made Windows PowerShell a popular scripting shell. Furthermore, with the release of Windows Server 2012 and Windows 8, Windows PowerShell version 3.0 was a drastic improvement in terms of the number of cmdlets and modules. They have also introduced the Windows PowerShell Web Access (PWA), PowerShell Workflows, and Scheduled Jobs concept in this version. The exciting part is that while we were drafting this book, the Microsoft team was coming up with its next release of operating systems, named Windows Server 2012 R2 and Windows 8.1. In this release, they have introduced Windows PowerShell v4.0 embedded with extensive functionality, such as **Desired State Configuration (DSC)** and so on.

 While we are in the process of publishing this book, the PowerShell team has already come up with the preview release of Windows PowerShell 5.0 with some extensive functionality.

By default, Windows PowerShell 3.0 comes up with Windows Server 2012 and Windows 8. There are a number of default modules present in this version. If you are running an operating system lower than the ones specified in the preceding section, you need to manually install Windows Management Framework 3.0, which is also known as WMF 3.0.

 If you have installed any previous releases of Windows Management Framework, you must uninstall them before installing Windows Management Framework 3.0.

Windows Management Framework 3.0 can be installed only on the following operating system versions:

- Windows 7 SP1
- Windows Server 2008 R2 SP1 (WMF 3.0 is also supported if you are running Windows Server 2008 R2 as the server core)
- Windows Server 2008 SP2

Windows PowerShell 2.0 is embedded in the Windows Server 2008 R2 and Windows 7 operating system. You don't need to separately install it on these operating systems.

The contentions written here use the latest version of PowerShell (v 4.0). However, most of the cmdlets are also supported in the legacy version, as well. As a minimum, you need to have PowerShell 2.0 in your machine; however, it would be best to have the latest version of PowerShell. You can refer to the TechNet link (`https://technet.microsoft.com/en-us/library/hh847769.aspx`) for detailed information on the prerequisites for different versions of PowerShell.

Windows Management Framework 3.0 is available for all supported versions of Windows in the following languages: English, Chinese (simplified), Chinese (traditional), French, German, Italian, Japanese, Korean, Portuguese (Brazil), Russian, and Spanish.

Windows Management Framework 3.0 contains:

- Windows PowerShell 3.0
- **Windows Remote Management (WinRM)** 3.0
- **Windows Management Instrumentation (WMI)**
- Management OData IIS Extensions
- Server Manager CIM Provider

Windows Management Framework 3.0 requires the following software to be installed prior to the WMF 3.0 installation:

- **Microsoft .Net Framework 4.0**: You can install Microsoft .Net Framework at `http://go.microsoft.com/fwlink/?LinkID=212547`

- **Windows 7 Service Pack 1 on computers running Windows 7**: To install SP1, go to `http://www.microsoft.com/en-in/download/details.aspx?id=5842`

- **Windows Server 2008 R2 Service Pack 1 on computers running Windows Server 2008 R2**: To install SP1, go to `http://www.microsoft.com/en-in/download/details.aspx?id=5842`

- **Windows Server 2008 Service Pack 2 on computers running Windows Server 2008**: To install SP2, go to `http://www.microsoft.com/en-in/download/details.aspx?id=16468`

In addition to the preceding software, you will need to meet the following requirements:

- To install Windows PowerShell Integrated Scripting Environment (ISE) for Windows PowerShell 3.0 on computers running Windows Server 2008 R2 with Service Pack 1, use Server Manager to add the optional Windows PowerShell ISE feature to Windows PowerShell before installing WMF 3.0.

- Install the latest updates before installing WMF 3.0.

 WMF 4.0 has the same set of OS requirement, but it needs Microsoft .Net Framework 4.5 as a prerequisite.

Setting up the System Center Configuration Manager environment

This section talks about how to setup your Windows PowerShell console to start with the SCCM activities. The traditional method of importing the SCCM module in Windows PowerShell is supported by SCCM 2007 and its later versions.

The prerequisites to set up SCCM are as follows:

- SCCM 2007 or its later version infrastructure
- Windows PowerShell 2.0 or its later version

Connecting to Windows PowerShell for SCCM

The steps for connecting to Windows PowerShell for SCCM are as follows:

1. Start the 32-bit Windows PowerShell console from your operating system box, as the SCCM infrastructure is only supported with the 32-bit PowerShell architecture.

2. If you are using Windows Server 2008 R2 or a similar operating system, then you can click on **Start**, search for **Windows PowerShell (x86)**, and launch the console.

   If you are using Windows Server 2012 or a similar operating system, then you can press the Windows key + *F*, search for **Windows PowerShell**, and choose **Apps** in the console. From the search list, select **Windows PowerShell (x86)** and launch the console.

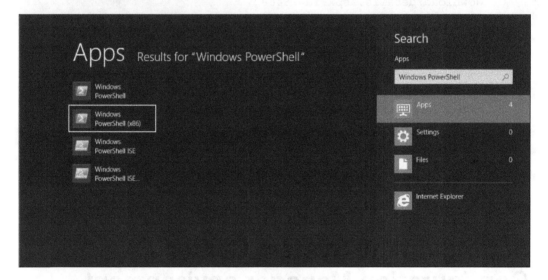

3. To import the Configuration Manager PowerShell module, we need to change the console location to the `Configuration Manager Installation` folder. For example, we will refer to the parent installation folder as `C:\Program Files(x86)`.

4. Type the following lines into the PowerShell console:

   ```
   PS C :\> cd "C:\Program Files(x86)\Microsoft Configuration
   Manager\AdminConsole\bin"
   ```

   This will set the console location to the `bin` subfolder in the `Configuration Manager Installation` folder.

5. Now, import the `ConfigurationManger.psd1` module file by using the `Import-Module` cmdlet:

```
PS C :\> Import-Module .\ConfigurationManager.psd1
```

 To confirm the successful import of the module, you can type `Get-Module CMDLET` in the PowerShell console. Now you will be able to see the new module added to the **ConfigurationManager** list.

6. After successfully importing the module file, set the console location to your site location by using your site code. For example, we have taken ABC site code in the following command statement:

```
PS C :\> Set-Location ABC:
```

The Configuration Manager PowerShell module also includes PowerShell Driver Provider for Configuration Manager Sites. For example, if you have a central site administration, site `ABC` and two primary sites `PS1` and `PS2`, then you can change the connection context like this:

```
PS C :\> Set-Location ABC:
PS C :\> Set-Location PS1:
PS C :\> Set-Location PS2:
```

 If you don't change the connection context, then you can't manage the Configuration Manager Site as well.

7. Now you are ready to manage your Configuration Manager infrastructure using Windows PowerShell.

 Downloading the example code

You can download the example code files from your account at `http://www.packtpub.com` for all the Packt Publishing books you have purchased. If you purchased this book elsewhere, you can visit `http://www.packtpub.com/support` and register to have the files e-mailed directly to you.

There is also another simple method available to connect SCCM using PowerShell with the latest releases of SCCM 2012 and so on. The prerequisites for that are as follows:

- System Center Configuration Manager 2012 SP1 RTM or a later version infrastructure
- Windows Server 2012 or Windows Server 2008 R2 with WMF 3.0

Connecting to Windows PowerShell from the SCCM console

The steps for connecting to Windows PowerShell from the SCCM console are as follows:

1. Press the Windows key + *F*, search for **Configuration Manager**, and choose **Apps**. From the search list, select **Configuration Manager Console** and launch the console.

2. In the **Configuration Manager Console**, click on the upper-left corner of the console and select **Connect via Windows PowerShell**.

3. The Configuration Manager then imports the PowerShell module automatically.

4. Now you are ready to manage your Configuration Manager infrastructure using the Windows PowerShell console.

Setting up the System Center Operations Manager environment

This section discusses how to set up your PowerShell console to start with the SCOM activities. The traditional method of importing the SCOM module in Windows PowerShell is supported by SCOM 2012 and its later versions.

The prerequisites for this are as follows:

- SCOM 2012 or the later version infrastructure
- Windows PowerShell 2.0 or its later version

Connecting to Windows PowerShell for SCOM

The steps for connecting to Windows PowerShell for SCOM are as follows:

1. Start the 32-bit Windows PowerShell console from your operating system box.

2. If you are using Windows Server 2008 R2 or a similar operating system, then you can click on **Start,** search for **Windows PowerShell (x86)**, and launch the console.

3. If you are using Windows Server 2012 or a similar operating system, then you can press the Windows key + *F*, search for **Windows PowerShell**, and choose **Apps**. From the search list, select **Windows PowerShell (x86)** and launch the console.

4. To import the `Operations Manager PowerShell` module, we need to change the console location to the `Operations Manager Console installation` folder. For example, we will refer to the parent installation folder as `C:\Program Files(x86)`.

   Type the following lines into the PowerShell console:

   PS C :\> cd 'C:\Program Files\System Center 2012\Operations Manager\PowerShell\'

5. This will set the console location to the `PowerShell` subfolder in the `Operations Manager Console` installation folder.

6. Now, import the `OperationsManger.psd1` module file by using the `Import-Module` cmdlet:

   PS C :\> Import-Module .\OperationsManager.psd1

 To confirm the successful import of the module, type the `Get-Module` cmdlet on the PowerShell console. Now you will be able to see the new module added to the `OperationsManager` list.

7. Now you are ready to manage your Operations Manager infrastructure, using the Windows PowerShell console.

Setting up the System Center Service Manager environment

In this section, we will talk about how to set up your PowerShell console to start with the SCSM activities. The traditional method of importing the SCSM module in Windows PowerShell is supported by SCSM 2010 and its later versions.

Here are the prerequisites to set up the SCSM environment:

* SCSM 2010 or its later version infrastructure
* Windows PowerShell 2.0 or its later version

Connecting to Windows PowerShell for SCSM

1. Start the Windows PowerShell console from your operating system box.

2. If you are using Windows Server 2008 R2 or a similar operating system, then you can click on **Start**, search for **Windows PowerShell (x86)**, and launch the console.

3. If you are using Windows Server 2012 or a similar operating system, then you can press the Windows key + *F*, search for **Windows PowerShell**, and choose **Apps**. From the search list, select **Windows PowerShell (x86)** to launch the console.

4. To import the `Service Manager PowerShell` module, we need to change the console location to the `Service Manager Console installation` folder. For example, we will refer to the parent installation folder as `C:\ Program Files(x86)`.

5. Type the following lines into the PowerShell console:

   ```
   PS C :\> cd 'C:\Program Files\Microsoft System Center 2012\Service Manager\'
   ```

   This will set the console location to the `Service Manager` subfolder in the `Service Manager Console installation` folder.

6. Import the `System.Center.Service.Manager.psd1` module file for SCSM Management Servers by using the `Import-Module` cmdlet:

   ```
   PS C :\> Import-Module .\System.Center.Service.Manager.psd1
   ```

7. Now you are ready to manage your Service Manager infrastructure for SCSM Management Servers using Windows PowerShell.

8. Import the `Microsoft.EnterpriseManagement.Warehouse.Cmdlets.psd1` module file for Data Warehouse Management Servers by using the `Import-Module` cmdlet:

   ```
   PS C :\> Import-Module .\Microsoft.EnterpriseManagement.Warehouse.
   Cmdlets.psd1
   ```

   To confirm the successful import of the module, you can type the `Get-Module` cmdlet on the PowerShell console. Now you will be able to see the new module added to the `System.Center.Service.Manager` and `Microsoft.EnterpriseManagement.Warehouse.Cmdlets` lists.

9. Now you are ready to manage your Service Manager infrastructure for Data Warehouse Management Servers using Windows PowerShell.

Summary

By end of this introductory chapter, you should be able to understand the basic terminology and setup requirement to use Windows PowerShell with several System Center products.

Going ahead, we will specifically look at each of these products and try to explore more functionalities that we can achieve using Windows PowerShell.

2
Administration of Configuration Manager through PowerShell

Now that we have the platform set up with Configuration Manager installed in our environment, it's time to understand how the collaboration of Configuration Manager and PowerShell can boost administration activities. We can always use the Configuration Manager console for administration activities (such as the traditional way of administration). However, there is another better and more efficient way for the GUI administration and that is through PowerShell. When we are required to automate a few activities in Configuration Manager, we need to use any of the scripting languages, such as VB or PowerShell. PowerShell has its own advantages over other scripting languages.

In this chapter, we will cover:

- The introduction of Configuration Manager through PowerShell
- Hierarchy details
- Asset and compliance
- Software distribution
- Operation system deployment
- Software update management

Introducing Configuration Manager through PowerShell

The main intention of this chapter is to give you a brief idea of how to use PowerShell with Configuration Manager and not to make you an expert with all the cmdlets. With the goal of introducing Configuration Manager admins to PowerShell, this chapter mainly covers how to use PowerShell cmdlets to get the information about Configuration Manager configurations and how to create our own custom configurations using PowerShell. Just like you cannot get complete information of any person during the first meet, you cannot expect everything in this chapter.

This chapter starts with an assumption that we have a well-built Configuration Manager environment. To start with, let's first understand how to fetch details from Configuration Manager. After that, we will create our own custom configurations. To stick on to convention, we will first learn how to fetch configuration details from Configuration Manager followed by a demonstration of how to create our own custom configurations using PowerShell.

PowerShell provides around 560 different cmdlets to administrate and manage Configuration Manager.

 You can verify the cmdlets counts for Configuration Manager by using the count operation with the Get-Command cmdlet with ConfigurationManager as the module parameter:

(Get-Command -Module ConfigurationManager).Count

It is always a good idea to export all the cmdlets to an external file that you can use as a reference at any point of time. You can export the cmdlets by using Out-File with the Get-Command cmdlet:

```
Get-Command -Module ConfigurationManager | Out-File "D:\SCCM\
PowerShellCmdlets.txt"
```

Once we have the Configuration Manager infrastructure ready, we can start validating the configurations through the PowerShell console. Here are the quick cmdlets that help to verify the Configuration Manager configurations followed by cmdlets to create custom configurations. Since PowerShell follows a verb-noun sequence, we can easily identify the cmdlets that help to check configurations as they start with `Get`. Similarly, cmdlets to create new configurations will typically start with `New`, `Start`, or `set`. We can always refer to the Microsoft TechNet page at `http://technet.microsoft.com/en-us/library/jj821831(v=sc.20).aspx` for the latest list of all the available cmdlets.

Before proceeding further, we have to set the execution location from the current drive to **System Center Configuration Manager** (**SCCM**) to avail the benefit of using PowerShell for the administration of SCCM. To connect, we can use the `Set-Location` cmdlet with the site code as the parameter or we can open PowerShell from the Configuration Manager console. Assuming we have `P01` as the site code, we can connect to Configuration Manager using PowerShell by executing the following command:

```
Set-Location P01:
```

Hierarchy details

This section will concentrate on how to get the Configuration Manager site details and how to craft our own custom hierarchy configurations using PowerShell cmdlets. This involves knowing and configuring the site details, user and device discovery, boundary configurations, and installation of various site roles.

Site details

First and foremost, get to know the Configuration Manager architecture details. You can use the `Get-CMSite` cmdlet to know the details of the Configuration Manager site. This cmdlet without any parameters will give the details of the site installed locally. To get the details of the remote site, you are required to give the site name or the site code of the remote site:

```
Get-CMSite

Get-CMSIte -SiteName "India Site"

Get-CMSite -SiteCode P01
```

Discovery details

It is important to get the discovery details before proceeding, as it decides the computer and the users that Configuration Manager will manage. PowerShell provides the Get-CMDiscoveryMethod cmdlet to get complete details of the discovery information. You can pass the discovery method as a parameter to the cmdlet to get the complete details of that discovery method. Additionally, you can also specify the site code as a parameter to the cmdlet to constrain the output of that particular site.

In the following example, we are trying to get the information of HeartBeatDiscovery and we are restricting our search to the P01 site:

```
Get-CMDiscoveryMethod -Name HeartBeatDiscovery -SiteCode P01
```

We can also pass other discovery methods as parameters to this cmdlet. Instead of HeartBeatDiscovery, you can use any of the following methods:

- ActiveDirectoryForestDiscovery
- ActiveDirectoryGroupDiscovery
- ActiveDirectorySystemDiscovery
- ActiveDirectoryUserDiscovery
- NetworkDiscovery

Boundary details

One of the first and most important and things to be configured in Configuration Manager are the boundary settings. Once the discovery is enabled, we are required to create a boundary and link it with the boundary group to manage clients through Configuration Manager.

PowerShell provides inbuilt cmdlets to get information of the configured boundaries and boundary groups. We also have the cmdlets to create and configure new boundaries.

You can use Get-CMBoundary to fetch the details of boundaries configured in Configuration Manager. PowerShell will also leverage you to use the Format-List attribute with the * (asterisk) wild character as the parameter value to get the detailed information of each boundary.

As default, this cmdlet will return and give you the available boundaries configured in Configuration Manager. This cmdlet will also accept parameters, such as the boundary name, which will give the information of a specified boundary. You can even specify the boundary group name as the parameter, which will return the boundary specified by the associated boundary group. You can also specify the boundary ID as a parameter for this cmdlet:

```
Get-CMBoundary -Name "Test Boundary"
Get-CMBoundary -BoundaryGroup "Test Boundary Group"
Get-CMBoundary -ID 12587459
```

Similarly, we can use `Get-CMBoundaryGroup` to view the details of all the boundary groups created and configured on the console. Using the cmdlet with no parameters will result in the listing of all the boundary groups available in the console. You can use the boundary group name or ID as a parameter to get the information of the interested boundary group:

```
Get-CMBoundaryGroup
Get-CMBoundaryGroup -Name "Test Boundary Group"
Get-CMBoundaryGroup -ID "1259843"
```

You can also get the information of multiple boundary groups by supplying the list as a parameter to the cmdlet:

```
Get-CMBoundaryGroup -Name "TestBG1", "TestBG2", "TestBG3", "TestBG4"
```

Until now, we saw how to read boundary and boundary-related details using PowerShell cmdlets. Now, let's see how to create our custom boundary in Configuration Manager using PowerShell cmdlets.

Just like you create boundaries in console, PowerShell provides the `New-CMBoundary` cmdlet to create boundaries using PowerShell. At the minimum, we are required to provide the boundary name, boundary type, and value as a parameter to the cmdlet.

We can create boundaries based on different criteria, such as the Active Directory site, IP subnet, IP range, and IPv6 prefix. PowerShell allows us to specify the criteria based on which we want to create a boundary in the boundary type parameter.

The following examples show you all four ways to create boundaries. The boundary type to be used is decided based on the architecture and the requirement:

```
New-CMBoundary -DisplayName "IPRange Boundary" -BoundaryType IPRange -Value "192.168.50.1-192.168.50.99"
New-CMBoundary -DisplayName "ADSite Boundary" -BoundaryType ADSite -Value "Default-First-Site-Name"
```

```
New-CMBoundary -DisplayName "IPSubnet Boundary" -BoundaryType IPSubnet -
Value "192.168.50.0/24"
```

```
New-CMBoundary -DisplayName "IPV6 Boundary" -BoundaryType IPv6Prefix -
Value "FE80::/64"
```

With the introduction of the boundary group concept with Configuration Manager 2012, it is expected that every boundary created should be made a part of a boundary group before it starts managing the clients. So, we first need to create a boundary group (if not present) and then add the boundary to the boundary group.

We can use the `New-CMBoundaryGroup` cmdlet to create a new Configuration Manager boundary group. At the minimum, we are required to pass the boundary group name as a parameter, but also it is recommended that you pass the boundary description as the parameter:

```
New-CMBoundaryGroup -Name "Test Boundary Group" -Description "Test
boundary group created from PowerShell for testing"
```

Upon successful execution, the command will create a boundary group named `Test Boundary Group`. We will now add our newly created boundary to this newly created boundary group. PowerShell provides an `Add-CMBoundaryToGroup` cmdlet to add the existing boundary to the existing boundary group:

```
Add-CMBoundaryToGroup -BoundaryName "IPRange Boundary" -BoundaryGroupName
"Test Boundary Group"
```

This will add the `IPRange Boundary` boundary to the `Test Boundary Group` boundary group. You can use looping to add multiple boundaries to the boundary group in a real-time scenario. We will discuss this scenario in depth in the next chapter of this book. We can remove a boundary from Configuration Manger using the `Remove-CMBoundary` cmdlet. We can just specify the name or ID of the boundary to be deleted as a parameter to the cmdlet:

```
Remove-CMBoundary -Name "Test Boundary" -force
```

Distribution point details

The details of the distribution points are one of the most common requirements, and it is essential that the Configuration Manager admin knows the distribution points configured in the environment to plan and execute any deployments. We can do this either using the traditional way of logging in to the console or by using the PowerShell approach. PowerShell provides the `Get-CMDistributionPoint` cmdlet to get the list of distribution points configured. Distribution points in Configuration Manager are used to store files, such as software packages, update packages, operating system deployment related packages, and so on.

If no parameters are specified, this cmdlet will list down all the distribution points available. You can pass the site server system name and site code as parameters to filter the result, which will restrict the results to the specified site:

```
Get-CMDistributionPoint -SiteSystemServerName "SCCMP01.Guru.Com" -
SiteCode "P01"
```

Here is a quick look of how to create and manage distribution points in Configuration Manager through PowerShell. We can create and manage the distribution point site system role in Configuration Manager through PowerShell just as we did using the console. To do this, we first need to create a site system server on the site (if not available), which we can later be upgraded as the site distribution point. We can do this using the New-CMSiteSystemServer cmdlet:

```
New-CMSiteSystemServer -sitecode "P01" -UseSiteServerAccount -ServerName
"dp.guru.com"
```

This will use the site server account for the creation of the new site system. Next, we will configure this site system as a distribution point. We can do this by using the Add-CMDistrubutionPoint cmdlet:

```
Add-CMDistributionPoint -SiteCode "P01" -SiteSystemServerName "dp.guru.
com" -MinimumFreeSpaceMB 500 -CertificateExpirationTimeUtc "2020/12/30" -
MinimumFreeSpaceMB 500
```

This will create dp.guru.com as a distribution point and also reserve 500 MB of space.

 We can also enable IIS and PXE support for the distribution point. We can also configure DP to respond to the incoming PXE requests with the following parameters. It just needs an extra effort to pass a few more parameters for the Distribution Point creation cmdlet:

```
Add-CMDistributionPoint -SiteCode "P01" -
SiteSystemServerName "dp.guru.com" -
MinimumFreeSpaceMB 500 -InstallInternetServer -
EnablePXESupport -AllowRespondIncomingPXERequest -
CertificateExpirationTimeUtc "2020/12/30"
```

We can create the distribution point group (if not already present) for the effective management of distribution point managements available in the environment using the New-CMDistributionPointGroup cmdlet with the minimum distribution point name as the parameter:

```
New-CMDistributionPointGroup -Name "Test Distribution Group"
```

With the distribution point group created, we can add the newly created distribution point to the distribution point group. You can use the `Add-CMDistributionPointToGroup` cmdlet with the distribution point name and distribution point group name, at the minimum, as parameters:

```
Add-CMDistributionPointToGroup -DistributionPointName "dp.guru.com" -
DistributionPointGroupName "Test Distribution Group"
```

We can also add any device collection to the newly created distribution point group so that whenever we deploy items (such as packages, programs, and so on) to the device collection, the content will be auto distributed to the distribution group:

```
Add-CMDeviceCollectionToDistributionPointGroup -DeviceCollectionName
"TestCollection1" -DistributionPointGroupName "Test Distribution Group"
```

Management point details

The management point provides polices and service location information to the client. It also receives data from clients and processes and stores it in the database. PowerShell provides the `Get-CMManagementPoint` cmdlet to get the details of the management point. Optionally, you can provide the site system server name and the site code as the parameter to the cmdlet.

The following example will fetch the management points associated with the `SCCMP01.Guru.Com` site system that has the site code `P01`:

```
Get-CMManagementPoint -SiteSystemServerName "SCCMP01.Guru.Com" -SiteCode
"P01"
```

When you install CAS or the primary server using the default settings, the distribution points and management points will be automatically installed. However, if you want to add an additional management point, you can add the role from the server or through the PowerShell console. PowerShell provides the `Add-CMManagementPoint` cmdlet to add a new management point to the site.

At the minimum, we are required to provide the site server name that we designated as the management point, database name, site code, the SQL server name, and the SQL instance name. The following example depicts how to create a management point through PowerShell:

```
Add-CMManagementPoint -SiteSystemServerName "MP1.Guru.Com" -SiteCode
"P01" -SQLServerFqDn "SQL.Guru.Com" -SQLServerInstanceName "SCCMP01"
-DataBaseName "SCCM" -ClientConnectionType InternetAndIntranet -
AllowDevice -GenerateAlert -EnableSsl
```

We can use the `Set-CMManagementPoint` cmdlet to change any management point settings that are already created.

The following example changes the `GenerateAlert` property to `false`:

```
Set-CMManagementPoint -SiteSystemServerName "MP1.Guru.Com" -SiteCode
"P01" -GenerateAlert:$False
```

Other site role details

Like distribution points and management points, we can get the detailed information of all other site roles (if they are installed and configured in the Configuration Manager environment). The following command snippet lists the different cmdlets available and their usage to get the details of different roles:

```
Get-CMApplicationCatalogWebServicePoint -SiteSystemServerName "SCCMP01.
guru.com" -SiteCode P01

Get-CMApplicationCatalogWebsitePoint -SiteSystemServerName "SCCMP01.guru.
com" -SiteCode P01

Get-CMEnrollmentPoint -SiteSystemServerName "SCCMP01.guru.com" -SiteCode
P01

Get-CMEnrollmentProxyPoint -SiteSystemServerName "SCCMP01.guru.com" -
SiteCode P01

Get-CMFallbackStatusPoint -SiteSystemServerName "SCCMP01.guru.com" -
SiteCode P01

Get-CMSystemHealthValidatorPoint -SiteSystemServerName "SCCMP01.guru.com"
-SiteCode P01
```

Asset and compliance

This section will mainly concentrates on gathering information and how to get details of devices, users, compliance settings, alerts, and so on. It also demonstrates how to create custom collections, add special configurations to collections, create custom client settings, install client agents, approve agents, and so on.

Collection details

Getting the collection details from PowerShell is as easy as using the console to get the details. You can use the `Get-CMDeviceCollection` cmdlet to get the details of the available collection. We can use the basics by using `Format-Table` with the `autosize` parameter to get the neat view:

```
Get-CMDeviceCollection | Format-Table -AutoSize
```

We can also use the grid view to get the details popped out as a grid. This will give us a nice grid that we can scroll and sort easily:

```
Get-CMDeviceCollection | Out-GridView
```

We can use `Name` or `CollectionID` as the parameter to get the information of a particular collection:

```
Get-CMDeviceCollection -Name "All Windows-7 Devices"
Get-CMDeviceCollection -CollectionId"2225000D"
```

You can also specify the distribution point group name as the parameter to get the list of the collection that is associated with the specified distribution point group:

```
Get-CMDeviceCollection -DistributionPointGroupName "Test Distribution
Point Group"
```

You can also replace the `DistributionPointGroupName` parameter with `DistributionPointGroupID` to pass the distribution point ID as a parameter to the cmdlet.

Similarly, you can use the `Get-CMUserCollection` cmdlet to get the details of the available user collection in SCCM:

```
Get-CMUserCollection | Format-Table -AutoSize
```

It is also possible to read direct members of any existing collection. PowerShell provides cmdlets to read the direct membership of both the device and user collection. We can use `Get-CMDeviceCollectionDirectMembershipRule` and `Get-CMuserCollectionDirectMembershipRule` to read the direct members of the device and user collection respectively:

```
CMDeviceCollectionDirectMembershipRule - CollectionName "Test Device
Collection" -ResourceID "45647936"
Get-CMUserCollectionDirectMembershipRule -CollectionName "Test User
Collection" -ResourceID 99845361
```

Similarly, PowerShell also empowers us to get the query membership rule by using the `Get-CMDevicecollectionQueryMembershipRule` and `Get-CMUsercollection QueryMembershipRule` cmdlets for the device and user collections respectively. The collection name and rule name needs to be specified as parameters to the cmdlet.

The following example assumes that there is already a collection named `All Windows-7 Machines` associated with the `Windows-7 Machines` rule name and an `All Domain Users` user collection associated with the `Domain Users` query rule:

```
Get-CMDeviceCollectionQueryMembershipRule -CollectionName "All Windows-7
Machines" -RuleName "Windows 7 Machines"

Get-CMUsercollectionQueryMembershipRule -CollectionName "All Domain
Users" -RuleName "Domain Users"
```

Reading Configuration Manager status messages

We can get status messages from one or more Configuration Manager site system components. A status message includes information of success, failure, and warning messages of the site system components. We can use the `Get-CMSiteStatusMessage` cmdlet to get the status messages. At the minimum, we are required to provide the start time to display the messages:

```
Get-CMSiteStatusMessage -ViewingPeriod "2015/02/20 10:12:05"
```

We can also include a few optional parameters that can help us to filter the output according to our requirement. Most importantly, we can use the computer name, message severity, and site code as additional parameters. For `Severity`, we can use the `All`, `Error`, `Information`, or `Warning` values:

```
Get-CMSiteStatusMessage -ViewingPeriod "2014/08/17 10:12:05" -
ComputerName XP1 -Severity All SiteCode P01
```

So, now we are clear on how to extract collection information from Configuration Manager using PowerShell. Let's now start creating our own collection using PowerShell.

Creating new user/device collections

Before you deploy any application, operating system, or client settings, you need to create the collection that is to be targeted. Just like in the console, PowerShell provides an easy way to create collections using cmdlets.

We can create the collection in SCCM with the `New-CMDeviceCollection` cmdlet. It is recommended that you give at least the basic, such as the name of the collection and the limiting collection ID:

```
New-CMDeviceCollection -Name "All Windows 8.1 Systems" -
LimitingCollectionID SMS00001
```

In the preceding example, we created the `All Windows 8.1 Systems` collection, which we are limiting to `All Systems`, which is represented in the collection ID.

Similarly, we can use the `New-CMUserCollection` cmdlet to create new user collections in Configuration Manager through PowerShell. At the minimum, we are required to provide the collection name and the limiting collection as parameters for the collection:

```
New-CMUserCollection -Name "Test User Collection" -LimitingCollectionName
"All Users"
```

Once the collection is created, we need to populate the collection with members. Here, we have two choices: to go for the direct membership rule (static rule) or to go with the query rule (dynamic membership). It depends on the scenario and the requirement as to which rule should be used.

In the following example, we will see how to populate the collection with the query membership rule. We can use the `Add-CMDeviceCollectionQueryMembershipRule` cmdlet to add membership rules to an existing device collection. At the minimum, you need to specify the collection name and query expression as parameters for the cmdlet:

```
Add-CMDeviceCollectionQueryMembershipRule -RuleName "All Windows 8.1
Systems" -Collectionname "All Windows 8.1 Systems" -QueryExpression
"select SMS_R_SYSTEM.ResourceType,SMS_R_SYSTEM.ResourceID,SMS_R_
SYSTEM.Name,SMS_R_SYSTEM.SMSUniqueIdentifier,SMS_R SYSTEM.
ResourceDomainORWorkgroup,SMS_R_SYSTEM.Client from sms_r_system where
OperatingSystemNameandVersion like '%6.3%'"
```

This will populate all the previously created `All Windows 8.1 Systems` collections with WQL, which will select all the machines that run the operating system version 6.3, which is the latest Windows client operating system, that is, Windows 8.

Similarly, we can add a query membership rule to the user of any existing collection using the `Add-CMUserCollectionQueryMembershipRule` cmdlet. At the minimum, we are required to provide the user collection name or ID, query expression, and the rule name as parameters to the cmdlet:

```
Add-CMUserCollectionQueryMembershipRule -CollectionName "Test User
Collection" -QueryExpression "Select SMS_R_User.ResourceID, SMS_R_User.
ResourceType, SMS_R_User.ResourceName, SMS_R_User.WindowsNTDomain  FROM
SMS_R_User " -RuleName "All Domain Users"
```

Adding a direct membership rule to the collection is one of the two ways to add members to an existing collection and is a static membership type (other being the query membership rule, which is dynamic).

PowerShell provides Add-CMDeviceCollectionDirectMembershipRulecmdlet to add direct members to the existing collection. At the minimum, we are required to provide the collection name and the resource ID as parameters:

```
Add-CMDeviceCollectionDirectMembershipRule -CollectionName "All Windows-8
Systems" -ResourceID 98574126
```

We can get the name of the resource ID of the Configuration Manager object using the Get-CMDevice cmdlet and by selecting only the resource ID parameter. In the following example, we try to get the resource ID of the SQL01 Configuration Manager object:

```
(Get-CMDevice -Name SQL01).ResourceID
```

Similarly, we can add the direct membership rule to the existing user collection using the Add-CMUserCollectionDirectMembershipRule cmdlet to add direct members to the existing Configuration Manager device collection. At the minimum, we are required to provide the user collection name and the resource ID as parameters to the cmdlet:

```
Add-CMUserCollectionDirectMembershipRule -CollectionName "Test User
Collection" -ResourceID 67474126
```

In a lab environment, once you are done with your testing or in a production environment, once you find that the collection is no more useful, it is recommended that you delete the collection. This is also a part of the Configuration Manager's maintenance job so that Configuration Manager is not overloaded with unnecessary objects. We can use the Remove-CMDeviceCollection cmdlet to remove or to delete the existing device collection from Configuration Manager. At the minimum, we are required to provide the collection name as a parameter to the cmdlet.

Similarly, we can use the Remove-CMUserCollection cmdlet to delete the user collections from Configuration Manager. Here also, we are required to pass the collection name to be deleted as a parameter to the cmdlet:

```
Remove-CMUserCollection -Name "Test User Collection" -Force
```

Handling Configuration Manager objects

Before we manage any device from Configuration Manager, we need to install a client agent on the client machine. We can install the Configuration Manager client using the PowerShell cmdlet, as we did using the traditional command-line style. PowerShell provides the `Install-CMClient` cmdlet to install the Configuration Manager client. As bare minimum, this cmdlet takes the machine name and site code as parameters, but requires additional parameters, such as whether to install on a domain controller or not, whether to force client installation all the time, and so on.

The following example shows the installation of the Configuration Manager client on the `Client1` machine with the site code `P01`:

```
Install-CMClient -DeviceName "Client1" -SiteCode "P01" -
AlwaysInstallClient $True -IncludeDomainController $False -ForceReinstall
$True
```

When the client is from a nontrusted domain, we have to manually approve the client in the Configuration Manager console to enable the client to join the site. PowerShell provides a cmdlet to automate the approval process, which will ease the administrator's life. You can use the `Approve-CMDevice` cmdlet to approve Configuration Manager clients. You are required to provide the device name as a parameter to the cmdlet. The following example shows how to approve the `Client1` machine:

```
Approve-CMDevice -DeviceName "Client1"
```

To add any object to an existing collection, it is important that we get the device or the user details available in the configuration database. PowerShell provides the `Get-CMDevice` and `Get-CMUser` cmdlet to get the device object and user object details in Configuration Manager.

The `Get-CMDevice` cmdlet accepts a wide range of parameters, such as the device name, device ID, collection name, and collection ID:

```
Get-CMDevice -Name XP1
```

Similarly, we can use `Get-CMUser` to get information of the user objects. This cmdlet works in the same way with `Get-CMDevice`:

```
Get-CMUser -Name "Guru\SMSSD"
```

Before we see the machine in all system collections, we are required to approve the machine after the client-agent installation. When we add any new device to Configuration Manager, PowerShell provisions us to approve the request without logging in to the console. We can use the `Approve-CMDevice` cmdlet that will accept one or more Configuration Manager clients join the site. The cmdlet accepts the device name or ID as a parameter:

```
Approve-CMDevice -DeviceName XP1
```

We can also block or unblock the Configuration Manager device objects for security reasons using the `Block-CMDevice` and `Unblock-CMDevice` cmdlets. The cmdlets will accept the device name or the device ID as a parameter and block/unblock the device:

```
Block-CMDevice -DeviceName XP1
Unblock-CMDevice -DeviceName XP1
```

The client settings information

We are well aware of the custom client settings and their importance in Configuration Manager. With the evolution of new versions, Configuration Manager provides full flexibility to control the device and user settings. Now, it is so flexible that we can create different custom client settings for each different collection to have maximum control over the clients. These settings will determine the way the clients interact with the management-point-like client policy polling interval in seconds, agent behavior, endpoint protection details, hardware and software inventory settings, software update settings, and so on.

We can use the `Get-CMClientSetting` cmdlet to get the details of all the client settings present in Configuration Manager. If no parameters are specified, the cmdlet will retrieve details of all the client settings present in Configuration Manager. We can pass the name of the client setting as a parameter to restrict the output to our desired settings:

```
Get-CMClientSetting
Get-CMClientSetting -Name "Win-7 Client Settings"
```

We can also create our own custom client settings using PowerShell. The following example will explain how to create a new custom client setting and deploy it to a test collection. Custom client settings have higher priority over default settings. Until the custom settings are deployed on any collection, the custom settings will have no effect on the environment.

Here, we are creating a custom client setting named `Custom Settings for Testing`. We can use the `New-CMClientSetting` cmdlet to create new custom client settings:

```
New-CMClientSetting -Name "Custom Settings for Testing" -Type Device -
Description "This is a custom client setting created using PowerShell"
```

Once you create the custom client setting, you are required to customize the settings according to your requirements. You can use the `Set-CMClientSetting` cmdlet to customize the existing custom client settings.

To do this, first we will add `Client Polices` to the custom settings, such as policy polling interval, enabling and disabling policies on the client, and policy request from Internet clients:

```
Set-CMClientSetting -Name "Custom Settings for Testing" -
PolicyPollingInterval 45 -EnableUserPolicyPolling $True -
EnableUserPolicyOnInternet $False
```

Next, we will add the `Computer Agent` settings to the newly created custom client settings:

```
Set-CMClientSetting -Name "Custom Settings for Testing" -
PowerShellExecutionPolicy ByPass -Initial Reminder HoursInterval 50
-Interim Reminder HoursInterval 5 -Final Reminder MinutesInterval
15 -PortalUrl http://SCCMP01.guru.com/CMApplicationCatalog
-AddPortalToTrustedSite $True - DisplayNewProgramNotification $True
```

Once the custom client settings are created, the settings will not have any effect until you deploy the client settings to a collection. Now, we will deploy the newly created custom client settings to all Windows 8 machines. Before deploying the client settings in this scenario, we are required to create a collection with all Windows 8 machines if one is not already present:

```
Start-CMClientSettingDeployment -ClientSettingName "Custom Settings for
Testing" -CollectionName "All Windows-8 Systems"
```

Alert management

Configuration Manager is capable of self-monitoring and equipped with a dashboard, which shows alerts whenever something goes wrong in the Configuration Manager environment. First, let's look at the cmdlet that will get the alerts registered without logging in to the console. PowerShell provides the `Get-CMAlert` cmdlet to fetch the details of all the alerts registered.

If we use the cmdlet without any parameters, the cmdlet will return the list of all the alerts registered. We can also use a parameter-like partial name of the alert or the alert ID to get the details of a particular alert:

```
Get-CMAlert
Get-CMAlert -Name "*Software*"
Get-CMAlert -id 147*
```

The second cmdlet will list all the alerts that have the `Software` keyword in them. This will allow us to filter the alerts according to our requirements. This cmdlet can be integrated with the pipeline option available with PowerShell for the best utilization of the cmdlet.

To make our life easier while monitoring the alerts, we can subscribe to particular alerts. We will discuss how to create alert subscriptions in the next chapter; for now, let's see how to view the list of available subscription using PowerShell. PowerShell provides the `Get-CMAlertSubscription` cmdlet to view the list of alert subscriptions in Configuration Manager and its property.

We can directly use the cmdlet to get all the alerts subscribed in the console or we can give the name of the subscription as the parameter to the cmdlet to get complete details of that particular subscription:

```
Get-CMAlertSubscription
Get-CMAlertSubscription -Name "Software Distribution Failure Alerting Group"
Get-CMAlertSubscription -ID 147*
```

Software distribution

This section provides detailed knowledge of how to get information of software distribution components (including information on packages, programs, applications, and so on) and how to create your own package, program, and applications using PowerShell cmdlets. This section will also cover how to distribute and deploy packages and applications using PowerShell.

Handling packages and applications

PowerShell allows you to get details of one or more packages in Configuration Manager. You can use the package name and package ID as parameters to the cmdlet. If no parameters are specified, the cmdlet will retrieve all the packages available in Configuration Manager:

```
Get-CMPackage -Name "Adobe Reader"
```

We can use `Get-CMApplication` to get the details of all the applications available in the Configuration Manager database. If no parameters are specified, the cmdlet will retrieve all the applications available in the database:

```
Get-CMApplication
```

For any reason, if we are required to suspend the application, PowerShell provides `Suspend-CMApplication` to achieve the task. We are required to send the application ID as a parameter to cmdlet:

```
Suspend-CMApplication -ID "1574263"
```

To resume the suspended application, we can use the `Resume-CMApplication` cmdlet. Once we resume the application, the clients will start downloading the application:

```
Resume-CMApplication -ID "1574263"
```

Once the package is no more of use to us, we can delete the Configuration Manager package by using `Remove-CMPackage`. Once the package is deleted, all traces of the package are removed even from child sites. We can identify the package to be deleted by passing the package ID as a parameter to the cmdlet.

Similarly, we can remove the Configuration Manager application using the `Remove-CMApplicaton` cmdlet:

```
Remove-CMApplication -ID "1574263"
Remove-CMPackage -ID "CM10000F"
```

Now that we have the basic knowledge of package and application handling, we can proceed with the creation of package and applications through PowerShell.

PowerShell will provide the cmdlet to create applications in the same way we created them from the console. PowerShell provides `New-CMApplication` to create the Configuration Manager application through a command line. The following example shows how to create an application through the PowerShell cmdlet:

```
New-CMApplication -Name "Win Zip App" -Description "Win Zip App
created through PowerShell" -LocalizedApplicationName "Win Zip App" -
LocalizedApplicationDescription "Win Zip App For Windows 8" -AutoInstall
$True -Owner "Win Zip" -SoftwareVersion "V7.2"
```

Once the application is created, the additional parameters can be set using the `Set-CMApplication` cmdlet. In case you forget to specify the application description or the auto-installation property during the application or if you would like to modify the values, `Set-CMApplication` will assist you on this:

```
Set-CMApplication -Name "Win Zip App" -DistributionPriority High -Keyword
Zip
```

Creating the package is the first step of the distribution of software in the traditional way (as in SCCM 2007). This process is still supported in the new version of Configuration Manager. Configuration Manager supports the `New-CMPackage` cmdlet to create a new package in SCCM using PowerShell. We are required to provide the package name and the content path as parameters to the cmdlet:

```
New-CMPackage -Name "Win Zip PS" -Description "Win Zip Package Created
From PowerShell" -Version "8.0" -Path "\\SCCMP01\D$\Package\SD\Win Zip"
```

Once the package is created, we are required to set a few of the mandatory properties to the package. PowerShell provides the `Set-CMPackage` cmdlet to set the custom settings to the package. At the minimum, the cmdlet will accept the name as the parameter and the additional parameter to add custom settings to the package.

In this example, we have set the number of retry options and the priority for package distribution. You can set many other options as per your requirements:

```
Set-CMPackage -Name "Win Zip PS" -Language "English" -
ForcedDisconnectNumberRetries 10 -DistributionPriority High
```

Handling programs

It is possible to get the details of one or more programs in Configuration Manager. Configuration Manager allows you to associate multiple programs with the same package. If no parameters are specified, the cmdlet will list all the programs available in the console. You can associate the package ID and the program name as parameters to the cmdlet.

In the following example, we see that the cmdlet is trying to retrieve information from the `Win Zip - 7` program in the package with the `ST100026` ID:

```
Get-CMProgram -PackageID "ST100026" -ProgramName "Win Zip - 7"
```

PowerShell will also provide us the way to enable and disable the programs that are already created. PowerShell provides `Disable-CMProgram` to disable one or more Configuration Manager programs. Once the program is disabled, Configuration Manager will stop the program on the client. When we disable the program, Configuration Manager still pushes the program to the distribution point and advertises this to the client. It is just that the program will fail to run at the client end. Like `Get-CMProgram`, this cmdlet also accepts the package ID and program name as parameters for execution.

You can use the `Enable-CMProgram` cmdlet to enable the disabled programs in order to resume execution. This cmdlet also accepts the package ID and program name as parameters:

```
Disable-CMProgram -PackageID "ST100026" -ProgramName "Win Zip -7"
Enable-CMProgram -PackageID "ST100026" -ProgramName "Win Zip -7"
```

PowerShell provides the `Remove-CMProgram` cmdlet to delete one or more programs once the program is not useful anymore. Once the package is removed, Configuration Manager will remove all the advertisements associated with the program. PowerShell provides a direct way to delete the program by passing the package ID and program name as parameters:

```
Remove-CMProgram -PackageID "ST100026" -ProgramName "Win Zip - 7"
```

Now, we are familiar with the reading program details using PowerShell cmdlets. Let's see how to create a new package using PowerShell. We will resume from the point where we created our custom package before; once we customize our package, we need to create a program for our package. PowerShell provides the `New-CMProgram` cmdlet to create programs in SCCM. At the minimum, the cmdlet will accept the package name, program name, and command line as the parameters.

The following command will create a program with the run type as `hidden`. We will configure the program to run it irrespective of whether the user is logged in or not. Additionally, you can also set the program to run the administrative rights or any other execution account and prerequisite specification, such as disk space (`-diskspaceunit`), drive letter (`-driveletter`), and so on:

```
New-CMProgram -PackageName "Win Zip PS" -StandardProgramName "Win Zip
PS - Program" -CommandLine "msiexec.exe /q /norestart" -Runtype Hidden -
ProgramRunType "WhetherOrNotUserIsLoggedOn"
```

Handling deployment types

First, let's try reading the deployment types available and preconfigured in Configuration Manager followed by creating our own custom deployment types. PowerShell provides the `Get-CMDeployment` cmdlet to view the deployment details of one or more deployments. Deployment is of an application or software update packages. If no parameters are specified, the cmdlet will get all the deployments available in the database. We can get the details of a particular deployment by passing the deployment ID as a parameter:

```
Get-CMDeployment -DeploymentID "CM1000256"
```

Also, we can use `Get-CMDeploymentPackage` to get the details of package deployments of a distribution point. At the minimum, the package accepts the distribution point name as the parameter and accepts the deployment package name as an optional parameter:

```
Get-CMDeploymentPackage -DistributionPointName "SCCMDP2.Guru.Com"
```

You can also get the status of one or more software distribution deployments using the `Get-CMDeploymentStatus` cmdlet. At the minimum, the cmdlet will accept the deployment name or ID as a parameter:

```
Get-CMDeploymentStatus -Name "Test Deployment"
```

We can also get information of the deployment type associated with the deployment using the `Get-CMDeploymentType` cmdlet. The deployment type specifies the rule for the deployment of software. At the minimum, we are required to provide the application name or application ID as a parameter to the cmdlet:

```
Get-CMDeploymentType -ApplicationName "Test Application"
```

Now, let's see how to create our own deployment types using PowerShell. We can create a deployment type for the application in the same way we did for the package. You can use the same `Add-CMDeploymentType` cmdlet with the application name as a parameter instead of the package name:

```
Add-CMDeploymentType -ApplicationName "Test Application" -MsiInstaller -
AutoIdentifyFromInstallationFile -InstallationFileLocation "\\SCCMP01\
Softwares\Application\Webapp.msi" -ForceForUnknownPublisher 1
```

Once the package and program are created, we are required to distribute the contents to the distribution point or the distribution point group. We can use the `Start-CMContentDistribution` cmdlet to distribute the contents to the desired DP or DP group:

```
Start-CMContentDistribution -PackageName "Win Zip PS" -
DistributionPointGroupName "Test Distribution Group"
```

Handling application or package deployment

Once the contents are distributed (such as an application), the next step is to deploy the application to the collection so that all the collection members receive your application. You can use the `Start-CMApplicationDeployment` cmdlet with the collection name, application name, and other custom.

The following example will demonstrate how to deploy the Win Zip application to the Test Collection collection:

```
Start-CMApplicationDeployment -CollectionName "Test Collection" -
Name "Win Zip" -comment "To deploy win zip for all systems in test
collections" -RebootOutsideServiceWindow $False -RaiseMomAlertsOnFailure
$True
```

As we can see in the preceding code, the cmdlet also accepts a few additional configurations that help the Configuration Manager admins to exercise granular control on the application deployment.

Creating an application catalog web service point and application catalog website point roles

We can create SCCM site roles in Configuration Manager through PowerShell in the same way we did from the console. In this example, we will see how to create the application catalog web service and application catalog website point though PowerShell.

PowerShell provides the Add-CMApplicationCatalogWebServicePoint cmdlet to create and configure the application catalog web service point. At the minimum, you are required to provide parameters, such as the port number for communication, site code, site system server name, IIS website name, and communication type as HTTP or HTTPS. The following example shows how to create an application catalog web service point:

```
Add-CMApplicationCatalogWebServicePoint -PortNumber 80 -SiteCode "P01"
-SiteSystemServerName "SCCMP01.guru.com" -CommunicationType HTTP -
IISWebSite "Default Web Site"
```

Once the application catalog web service point is set, the next step is to create and configure the application catalog website point. PowerShell provides the Add-CMApplicationCatalogWebsitePoint cmdlet to create and configure the application catalog website point. As a minimum, we are required to supply the site system server name, site code, application catalog web server point details, port number for communication, whether to configure as HTTP or HTTPS connection, web application name, organization name, and the color details:

```
Add-CMApplicationCatalogWebSitePoint -SiteSystemServerName
"SCCMP01.guru.com" -PortForHttpConnection 80 -SiteCode "ASC"   -
ConfiguredAsHTTPConnection -IISWebsite "Default Web Site" -
Organization "Guru Lab" -NetBIOSName "SCCMP01" -ColorBlue 52
-SiteSystemServerNameConfiguredForApplicationCatalogWebServicePoint
"SCCMP01.guru.com"
```

We can delete the application catalog website point and application catalog web service point using the `Remove-CMApplicationCatalogWebsitePoint` and `Remove-CMApplicationCatalogWebServicePoint` cmdlet, respectively. We are required to pass the site code and site system server name as the parameter name to the cmdlet. The following examples demonstrate the usage of the cmdlets in these cases:

```
Remove-CMApplicationCatalogWebsitePoint -SiteCode "P01" -
SiteSystemServerName "SCCMP01.guru.com"

Remove-CMApplicationCatalogWebServicePoint -SiteCode "P01" -
SiteSystemServerName "SCCMP01.guru.com"
```

The operating system deployment

This section will shed light on how to view details of the operating system deployment process and configurations, such as the boot image, operating system image files, task sequence, and so on.

An operating system image

Operating system images are the `.wim` files that are used for the operating system capture and deployment process. PowerShell will provide you the mechanism to extract the available operating system image files in Configuration Manager. We can use the `Get-CMOperatingSystemImage` cmdlet to list all the images.

Without parameters, the cmdlet will list all the images available in Configuration Manager. You can pass the image name or ID as a parameter to get details of a particular image:

```
Get-CMOperatingSystemImage -Name "Boot image (x86)"
```

We can add a new operating system image to Configuration Manager by using the `New-CMOperationSystemImage` cmdlet. At a minimum, we are required to provide the name of the image file and the path to that file. Optionally, we can also pass the description, which holds a short description of the image file, as a parameter. The following example demonstrates how to import the operating system image to the Configuration Manager database:

```
New-CMOperatingSystemImage -Name "Goldan Win_8" -Path "\\SCCMP01\Images\
Boot.wim"
```

Operating system installers

An operating system installer is the installation file that contains all the necessary files that Configuration Manager needs to install on the operating system on any reference computer. PowerShell provides the `Get-CMOperatingSystemInstaller` cmdlet to get information of operating system installers. If no parameters are specified, the cmdlet will return all the available installers present in Configuration Manger. We can pass the installer name or ID as a parameter to streamline the output:

```
Get-CMOperatingSystemInstaller -Name "Win-7 Package"
```

We can add the operating system installer to Configuration Manager using the `New-CMOperatingSystemInstaller` cmdlet. At the minimum, we need to pass the name of the installer and the path to the installer as parameters to the cmdlet. Optionally, we can also specify the description and version as parameters to the cmdlet. The following example demonstrates how to import the operating system installer to Configuring Manager using the PowerShell cmdlet:

```
New-CMOperatingSystemInstaller -Name "CustomInstaller" -Path "\\SCCMP01\
Win8"
```

We can use the `Set-CMOperatingSystemInstaller` cmdlet to change any configurations of the existing operating system installer. At the minimum, we are required to specify the name or the ID of the operating system installer that is to be modified followed by the necessary modifications:

```
Set-CMOperatingSystemInstaller -Name "CustomInstaller" -NewName
"NewCustomInstaller" -Version "1.1"
```

We can remove the unused operating system installers from Configuration Manager using the `Remove-CMOperatingSystemInstaller` cmdlet. At the minimum, we are required to pass the name or the ID of the operating system installer image that is to be deleted:

```
Remove-CMOperatingSystemInstaller -Name "CustomInstaller" -Force
```

Boot image details

Operating system boot images are `.wim` for file, which has files and folders that are essential to install and configure an operating system. Configuration Manager will have boot images for both X86 and X64. We can create our own custom boot images as per our requirements. PowerShell provides the `Get-CMBootImage` cmdlet to view the boot images loaded on Configuration Manager. If no parameter is specified, the cmdlet will return all the boot images present in the database. We can pass the boot image ID or name to get the details of a particular boot image:

```
Get-CMBootImage -Name "Windows-7 Gloden"
```

PowerShell provides the `Remove-CMBootImage` cmdlet to delete unwanted boot images in the console. The ID of the boot image to be deleted must be passed as the parameter to the cmdlet:

```
Remove-CMBootImage -ID "Boot image (x86)"
```

Handling drivers for deployments

The task sequence for the operating system deployment contains device drivers. We can use the `Get-CMDriver` cmdlet to get the list of the driver software present in the console. If no parameters are specified, the cmdlet will retrieve all the driver software uploaded to Configuration Manager. We can pass the driver name, driver package name, or the package ID as a parameter to get complete information of a particular driver software:

```
Get-CMDriver

Get-CMDriver -DriverPackageName "Print Drivers"
```

We can disable and enable the drivers in Configuration Manager using the `Disable-CMDriver` and `Enable-CMDriver` cmdlets, respectively:

```
Disable-CMDriver -Name "cdrom.inf"

Enable-CMDriver -Name "cdrom.inf"
```

Also, you can delete the driver from the Configuration Manager database using the `Remove-CMDriver` cmdlet. This cmdlet will accept, at a minimum, the name or the ID of the driver to be deleted as a parameter:

```
Remove-CMDriver -Name "cdrom.inf"
```

PowerShell also enables you to get all the driver packages available in the Configuration Manager database using the `Get-CMDriverPackage` cmdlet. If no parameters are specified, the cmdlet will return all the driver packages available. We can restrict the output by passing the package name or the package ID we are interested in:

```
Get-CMDriverPackage -ID "CM100027"
```

We can create our own custom driver package using the `New-CMdriverPackage` cmdlet. At the minimum, we need to pass the package name and package source type as parameters to the cmdlet. The `PackageSourcetype` parameter specifies the method to read the package source file. We can use `StorageCompress`, `StorageDirect`, `StorageLocal`, `StorageNeedsSpecifying` or `StorageNOSource` as values to the parameter:

```
New-CMDriverPackage -Name "Package1" -Path "\\SCCMP01\Drivers" -
PackageSourcetype Storagelocal
```

We can change the configurations of the existing driver package using the `Set-CMDriverPackage` cmdlet. We are required to provide the name or the ID of the driver package followed by the changes to be incorporated.

We can remove any particular driver from the driver package using the `Remove-CMDriverFromDriverPackage` cmdlet. At the minimum, we need to pass the driver ID to be deleted and the package name or ID from which the driver is to be deleted:

```
Remove-CMDriverFromDriverPackage -DriverName "Display VGI Driver" -
DriverPackageName "Package1" -Force
```

Also, we can use `Remove-CMDriverPackage` to remove any driver package from the Configuration Manager database. At the minimum, the cmdlet requires the name or the ID of the package to be deleted as a parameter:

```
Remove-CMDriverPackage -ID "CM100027"
```

Gathering the task sequence

The task sequence involves a sequence of steps to be executed during the deployment of any software or operating system. The task sequence is mainly used in operating system deployment to execute a predefined set of tasks. PowerShell allows us to get the task sequences available in the Configuration Manager console through the `Get-CMTaskSequence` cmdlet. If no parameters are specified, the cmdlet will return all the task sequences available within Configuration Manager. We can specify the name or the ID of a task sequence to get the complete details of a particular task sequence:

```
Get-CMTaskSequence -Name "Win-7 Deployment"
```

We can use the `Disable-CMTaskSequence` and `Enable-CMTaskSequance` cmdlet to disable and enable the existing task sequences, respectively. At the minimum, the cmdlets require the name of the task sequence to be disabled or enabled as the parameter:

```
Disable-CMTaskSequence -Name "Win-7 Deployment"
```

```
Enable-CMTaskSequence -Name "Win-7 Deployment"
```

We can use the `Remove-CMTaskSequence` cmdlet to remove the unused or unwanted task sequences from the configuration manger database:

```
Remove-CMTaskSequence -Name "Win-7 Deployment"
```

Software update management

PowerShell provides you cmdlets to get the details of software updates. This section covers cmdlets that we can use to update management activities.

Software catalog details

PowerShell provides you a way to list the software patches available in the Configuration Manager catalog using the `Get-CMSoftwareupdate` cmdlet. This will list all the updates present in the catalog with the default attributes:

```
Get-CMSoftwareUpdate
```

You can also query individual updates with the name of the patch as the attribute to the cmdlet. By specifying the name of the update, you can get complete details of the particular patch or update:

```
Get-CMSoftwareUpdate -Name "Cumulative Software Update for Internet Explorer"
```

We can also save the specified software update, which is part of the particular package, to a specified location:

```
Save-CMSoftwareUpdate -DeploymentPackageName "Finance Updates" -
SoftwareUpdateGroupName "Finance Package Updates" -Location "\\SCCMP01\
SP"
```

We can create a software update group that contains the group of updates we want to deploy. We can get the list of update groups available in Configuration Manger using the `Get-CMSoftwareUpdateGroup` cmdlet. With our parameters, the cmdlet will list all the available software update groups in Configuration Manager. We can specify the group name or ID to get detailed information of a particular group:

```
Get-CMSoftwareUpdateGroup
```

```
Get-CMSoftwareUpdateGroup -ID "P01000d"
```

```
Get-CMSoftwareUpdateGroup -Name "12"
```

By adopting the enhanced features in Configuration Manager, we can create automatic deployment rules for software updates depending on the requirements. We usually will not use automatic deployment rules to deploy security and application patches, as in production, we usually test the patches thoroughly before we implement them on the production servers. In some applications, such as antivirus patching, we may go for automatic deployment rules depending on the need.

PowerShell provides the `Get-CMSoftwareUpdateAutoDeploymentRule` cmdlet to retrieve information of auto deployment rules. If no parameters are specified, the cmdlet will return the details of all the auto deployment rules in Configuration Manager. We can send the name or ID of the specific auto deployment rule to get the details of a particular rule:

```
Get-CMSoftwareUpdateAutoDeploymentRule
Get-CMSoftwareUpdateAutoDeploymentRule -Name "Antivirus updates"
Get-CMSoftwareUpdateAutoDeploymentRule -ID "1257625"
```

PowerShell will provide an additional cmdlet to get the details of the software update packages in Configuration Manager. We can use `Get-CMSoftwareUpdateDeploymentPackage` to get the details of the software update packages. If no parameters are specified, the cmdlet will return all the software update packages present in Configuration Manager. As with the other cmdlets, we can pass the name or ID of the required software update package to sharpen the output according to our requirement:

```
Get-CMSoftwareUpdateDeploymentPackage
Get-CMSoftwareUpdateDeploymentPackage -Name "All Security Updates"
Get-CMSoftwareUpdateDeploymentPackage -ID 1257486
```

Summary

By now, you should be familiar with how to use PowerShell to get the basic details of the Configuration Manager environment, have an idea of how PowerShell displays the output, and know how to export the output to a file, so that it is used for reporting or is kept for later usage.

You should be familiar with how to create your own custom client settings and how to modify existing configurations. With this assumption, we will see some real-time scenarios that will help us to understand cmdlet's usage better. In the next chapter, we will look at some real-time SCCM administration scenarios and the usage of PowerShell cmdlets to handle tasks.

Scenario-based Scripting for SCCM Administration

Now that we have a basic understanding of how to use PowerShell cmdlets with Configuration Manager, it is time to better understand its real-time concepts. This chapter contains a few scenario-based examples that can help you to get an idea of the real power of PowerShell when used with Configuration Manager.

In this chapter, we will cover the following scenarios:

- Adding multiple distribution points to a distribution point group
- Creating multiple packages with the .csv/.txt file input
- Using PowerShell to access the Configuration Manager installation directory
- Checking for SCCM services
- Operating a system deployment precheck
- Running a ping test
- Getting a list of primary sites in the Configuration Manager environment
- Getting a list of all the site servers in the Configuration Manager environment
- Getting component status in Configuration Manager

Installing the SCCM client agent version. The code blocks demonstrated in this chapter will not include error-handling mechanisms. When using the code in real-time scenarios, it is very important to include error-handling mechanisms to handle errors in a well-structured way.

For a better understanding of the code blocks used, you can try them in your lab environment and analyze the output. Try to modify the output according to your requirements. This will give you the confidence to write and implement these codes in the production environment. Before implementing any code block in production, make sure you have thoroughly tested the code in the development or test environment. Once you have satisfactorily tested the code in the development environment, move the code to the preproduction environment and test for its truthiness. Once you are sure that the script is working perfectly and delivering the expected results, implement it in the production environment.

Scenario 1 – adding multiple distribution points to a distribution point group

This is one common scenario where Configuration Manager administrators are required to add multiple distribution points to a **distribution point group (DP group)**. A text file with the distribution point list can be used as the input to the script.

Prescripting activities

Create a text file at D:\PowerShell\DPFile.txt (you can use your convenient location) and populate the file with the distribution points to be added to the DP group.

To show you a sample, DPFile.txt should contain DP names, as follows:

```
GURU.COM
DP1.GURU.COM
DP2.GURU.COM
```

Also, it is important to note that we should enter one DP name per line. Our sample file will look something like the following screenshot:

Assumption

We will assume the distribution point group is named Test Distribution Group and the text file location as D:\PowerShell. Look at the following code:

```
$FilePath = "D:\PowerShell\DPFile.txt"
$DPNames = Get-Content -path $FilePath
ForEach($DP in $DPNames)
{
  Add-CMDistributionPointToGroup -DistributionPointName $DP -
DistributionPointGroupName "Test Distribution Group"
Write-Host "Adding $dp to Test Distribution Group"
}
```

Each loop will take each DP one at a time from the list and add it to the Test Distribution Group DP group. On successful execution of the script, we can see that the multiple boundaries captured in the text file will be added to the Test Distribution Point DP group.

Scenario 2 – creating multiple packages with the .csv/.txt file input

This example covers the creation of multiple packages with the details present in the .txt file. Upon successful execution, we can see multiple packages created in the Configuration Manager console with the details or configurations present in the input file.

Prescripting activities

We are required to create a `.csv` file with the details of each package that will be created. The details include the name of the packages, the manufacturer and version, and the description and the path of the source file, with the file located in the `D:\SCCM` folder. For reference, let's name the `Package.csv` file. For the current example, we will take an example file with contents, as shown in the following screenshot:

A	B	C	D	E	F
Name	Description	Manufactu	Version	Path	
Pack1	This is pack1	abc	1.3	\\win2012r2.ahcheng.local\shared\pack1	
Pack2	This is pack2	xyz	8.6	\\win2012r2.ahcheng.local\shared\pack2	
Pack3	This is pack3	klm	7.2	\\win2012r2.ahcheng.local\shared\pack3	

Consider the following code:

```
$PkgDetails = Import-csv -path "D:\SCCM\Package.csv"
Foreach($Pkg in $PkgDetails)
{
    $PkgName = $($Pkg.Name)
    $Description = $($Pkg.Description)
    $Mnfr = $($Pkg.Manufacturer)
    $Version = $($Pkg.Version)
    $Path = $($Pkg.Path)

    New-CMPackage -Name $PkgName -Description $Description -
Manufacturer $Mnfr -Version $Version -Path $Path
    Write-Host "Package $PkgName Created Successfully"
}
```

Scenario 3 – using PowerShell to get the Configuration Manager installation directory

One of the most common automation tasks that we carry out for Configuration Manager is the Configuration Manager health check framework. This primarily involves detecting the Configuration Manager installation directory.

It is not good practice to use the installation directory variable as static, but it is always advised that you make the variable dynamic, so that the script becomes more flexible and reusable. This example shows how PowerShell can be used to access the Configuration Manager installation directory:

```
Set-Location 'HKLM\SOFTWARE\Microsoft\SMS\Identification\ Installation
Directory'
$AllProp = Get-ItemProperty -path "HKLM\SOFTWARE\Microsoft\SMS\
Identification\ Installation Directory"
$InstallDir = $AllProp."Installation directory"
Write-Host "$InstallDir"
```

You can use `Set-Location` only if you are not specifying the full path for the `Get-ItemProperty` cmdlet. Here, we use the full path for both cmdlets to ensure that we get the required result even if we miss out setting the execution before reading the registry property.

For SCCM 2012 R2, the registry path would be `HKLM:\SOFTWARE\Microsoft\ ConfigMgr10\Setup\` and we will query for the `UI Installation Directory` item.

Scenario 4 – checking for SCCM services

Another common scenario when performing Configuration Manager health checks is to check for the existence of SCCM services, including the startup type and the status. We can create a function that receives the server name, service name, expected status, and expected startup type as parameters. It is recommended that you make changing variables parameters of the function so that we can make the function universal:

```
Function Get-ServiceStatus($ServerList, [string]$Servicename,
[string]$Status, [string]$Startup)
{
  foreach ($Comp in $ServerList)
  {
    if($Temp = Get-WmiObject Win32_Service -ComputerName $Comp |
where {$_.Name -eq $Servicename } | select Name, StartMode, State,
Displayname)
      {
        $Sname = $Temp.Displayname
        $ServiceState = $Temp.State
        $ServiceMode = $Temp.StartMode
        if(($ServiceState -eq $Status) -and ($ServiceMode -eq
$Startup))
          {
```

```
        Write-Host "service $Sname on $comp is Healthy" -
foregroundcolor "Green"
        }
      Else
      {
        Write-Host "service $Sname on $comp is not Healthy" -
foregroundcolor "Red"
        }
    }
    else
    {
        Write-Host "$ServiceName is not installed on $Comp" -
foregroundcolor "Red"
        }
    }
}
```

When we check for SCCM services, we can broadly classify the services into two categories, one is SCCM services and the other is SCCM-dependent services. The list of SCCM services depends on the roles installed, whereas the dependent services remain the same irrespective of the roles installed. Checking for a dependent service involves checking for the IIS service, WDS service, BITS service, and winmgmt service.

Here is the sample of how to call the function with the parameters included:

```
Get-serviceStatus "SCCMP01" "winMgmt" "Running" "Auto"
```

Scenario 5 – operating a system deployment precheck

One of the vital uses of Configuration Manager is the deployment of an operating system in large-scale enterprises. For successful operating system deployment, clients should have some of the prechecks completed successfully. One of the tests is for the existence of temp profiles in the machine. If temp profiles are present in a client machine, the chances of operating system deployment failure are more 'in both replace and refresh scenarios. The operating system deployment process fails even during the user-state capture step. So, it is good practice to automate prechecks using Configuration Manager before deploying the operating system.

One of the easiest ways to check for the existence of the temp profile is to check for the existence of the registry key. If the HKEY_LOCAL_MACHINE\SOFTWARE\Microsoft\ Windows\CurrentVersion\AccountPicture\Users registry key contains any of the sub keys with a .bkp extension, we can say that the computer has a temp profile in it, otherwise, we can confirm that the machine does not have any temp profile in it.

Pre-Scripting Activities: The following code will assume that we have a `complist.txt` text file that lists all the computer names to be migrated (which is supposed to undergo an operating system upgrade) and the text file is kept in the D drive.

Here is the sample `CompList.txt` file created for the script:

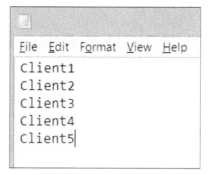

Check the following code:

```
$complist = Get-Content -Path "D:\PowerShell\Complist.txt"
foreach($comp in $complist)
{
   $sid = Invoke-Command -ComputerName $comp -ScriptBlock {

      Set-Location HKLM:

      Get-ChildItem -path "HKLM\SOFTWARE\Microsoft\Windows\
CurrentVersion\AccountPicture\Users" | Where-Object {$_.Name
-contains "bkp"}
   }
   if($sid -eq 0)
   {
     Write-Output "No temp profiles found in computer - $Comp"
   }
   else
   {
     Write-Output "Temp profiles found in computer - $Comp"
   }
}
```

This code will write on the console whether the computer has temp profiles in it or not. However, in real time, we can export the result on to any Excel, HTML, or CSV file for reporting. We usually integrate this code with other tests, and the overall result is reported in Excel, HTML, or CSV files. Then, the report is sent to deployment engineers for further actions.

Scenario 6 – running a ping test

Before doing any automation on the list of computers, the most important aspect to be tested is whether the computer is reachable or not. If the computer is offline, there is no point in running any automation script block on the computer. Executing script blocks on offline computers will just increase the script execution time. So, it is always advised that you perform a ping test on the list of computers we get as input and run the block of automation script only on the computers that are reachable.

Sometimes, server administrators disable ping on the server. This code works only if the ping is not disabled at the firewall level.

Prescripting activities

The following code assumes that we have a `complist.txt` file in the D drive, which contains the list of all the computer names that are to be tested whether they are reachable or not:

```
$CompList = Get-Content -Path "D:\PowerShell\Complist.txt"
foreach ($Comp in $CompList)
{
  If (test-Connection -ComputerName $Comp -Count 2 -Quiet)
  {
    Write-Host "server $Comp is reachable"
  }
  Else
  {
    Write-Host "server $Comp is not reachable"
  }
}
```

Scenario 7 – getting a list of primary sites in the Configuration Manager environment

As newbies to the Configuration Manager environment (though not new to Configuration Manager concepts), it is essential that we familiarize ourselves with its site design and implementation. We can list the available primary Configuration Manager sites in the environment by querying local **Windows Management Instrumentation (WMI)** of the **central administrative site (CAS)**. The following code will demonstrate how to query the CAS WMI to get the list of all the primary sites available in the Configuration Manager environment:

```
$PrimarySites = @()
$SiteCodeList = @()

$CentralSiteCode = "ABC"          # SCCM site code
$CentralSiteProvider = "SCCMCAS" # CAS server name

$Sites=Get-WmiObject -Namespace root\sms\site_$CentralSiteCode SMS_
Site -Filter "Type=2" -ComputerName $CentralSiteProvider
foreach ($site in $Sites)
{
  $SiteCode = $site.SiteCode.ToUpper()
  $SiteCodeList += $SiteCode
  $PrimarySites += $site
}
```

At the end of the execution, the `$SiteCodeList` array will have a list of the site codes of all the primary Configuration Manager servers configured in the environment, and the `$PrimarySites` variable will have a list of all the primary site servers configured.

Scenario 8 – getting a list of all site servers in the Configuration Manager environment

Once we know that the primary servers are installed in our environment, the next step is to identify the site servers that are installed in our environment. The following code demonstrates how to get the list of all site servers that are installed in our Configuration Manager environment:

```
$CentralSiteCode = "ABC"
```

```
$CentralSiteProvider = "SCCMCAS"

$SiteRoles = Get-WmiObject -ComputerName $CentralSiteProvider
-Namespace root\sms\site_$CentralSiteCode SMS_SystemResourceList
$Servers = new-object System.Collections.ArrayList
$ArrServers = new-object System.Collections.ArrayList
Foreach ($item in $SiteRoles)
{
    $StrFQDN = ($item.ServerRemoteName).ToUpper()

    $ArrServers.Add($StrFQDN) -
}
$Servers = $arrServers | sort | select -uniq
```

Upon successful execution of the code, the `$Servers` variable will have a list of all the site servers installed in the environment.

Scenario 9 – getting component status in Configuration Manager

It is always good to have a periodic check of the component status of the Configuration Manager components. The following code demonstrates how to get Configuration Manager components by querying WMI using PowerShell. To simplify the code, we will display the output on the console. However, in real-time practices, we usually capture the output in a reporting file. The following code will look for all the installed Configuration Manager components and verify the health of each component. The code will query the WMI for the `SMS_ComponentSummarizer` class to get the status of the site components:

```
$TallyInterval = "0001128000080008" #Since site installation
$CentralSiteCode = "ABC"
$CentralSiteProvider = "SCCMCAS"

$ComputersWithIssues = Get-WmiObject -Namespace root\sms\
Site_$CentralSiteCode -query "Select * from SMS_ComponentSummarizer
where Status <> 0 AND TallyInterval = '$TallyInterval'" -ComputerName
$CentralSiteProvider
Foreach ($CompStatus in $ ComputersWithIssues)
{
    switch ($CompStatus.state)
    {
        0 {$strState = "STOPPED"}
        1 {$strState = "STARTED"}
```

```
   2 {$strState = "PAUSED"}
   3 {$strState = "INSTALLING"}
   4 {$strState = "RE_INSTALLING"}
   5 {$strState = "DE_INSTALLING"}
   default {$strState = "UNKNOWN"}
}

Write-Host "---------------------------------------------"
Write-Host ("SiteCode:",$CompStatus.SiteCode)
Write-Host ("MachineName:",$CompStatus.MachineName)
Write-Host ("ComponentName:",$CompStatus.ComponentName)
Write-Host ("Errors:",$CompStatus.Errors)
Write-Host ("Warnings:",$CompStatus.Warnings)
Write-Host ("Infos:",$CompStatus.Infos)
Write-Host ("State:",$strState)
Write-Host "---------------------------------------------"

}
```

One of the parameters used for the query is `TallyInterval`. You can find more details on tally intervals at `https://msdn.microsoft.com/en-us/library/cc144112.aspx`.

Scenario 10 – installing the SCCM client agent version

It is a common requirement to pull out a report of the SCCM agent version installed on all the client machines in our Configuration Manager environment. This check can be considered one of the health check activities. The following code demonstrates how to get the client agent version installed on the list of computers.

Pre-Scripting Activities: Before we execute the script, we need to create a `CompList.txt` text file in the D drive (in case of different path, you can update the code block with the corresponding path) containing the list of computers on which the client agent version is to be extracted:

```
$Complist = Get-Content -Path "D:\CompList.txt"
foreach($Comp in $Complist)
{
  $SCCMClientVersion = (Get-WmiObject -Namespace root\ccm -Class CCM_
Client -ComputerName $Comp).ClientVersion
  Write-Host "SMS Client Agent Version For $Comp - $SCCMClientVersion"
}
```

Summary

This chapter gave a clear idea of the usage of PowerShell cmdlets in the real-time administration of Configuration Manager. We discussed various scenarios and the usage of PowerShell scripts to get the work done easily without human errors. You should now have a clear idea of how to use PowerShell cmdlets with SCCM 2012. In the next chapter, you will see how to manage another important product of the System Center family — System Center Operations Manager through PowerShell.

4

Administration of Operations Manager through PowerShell

In the last chapter, we saw the basic administration and management of Configuration Manager through PowerShell. Now, in this chapter, we will look at the administration and management of another very important product of the System Centre family, which is **System Center Operations Manager** (**SCOM**). SCOM is popularly known as Operations Manager.

In Configuration Manager, the entire content is divided in various subdivisions, which help us to better understand the consents:

- Monitoring
- Authoring
- Administration

Monitoring

This section covers **alert management**, **alert resolution**, and **alert filtering** in depth. It covers the real-time management of alerts and how to set up resolution states.

Knowing a management group

It is very important to know the management group details when you get into a new Operations Manager environment. PowerShell provides the `Get-SCOMManagementGroup` cmdlet to get the details of the infrastructure management group. We can also get the detailed information of the management servers available in our SCOM monitoring environment. We can use this cmdlet with no argument. This cmdlet will return the details of the current monitoring infrastructure, which includes the monitoring management group name and group-related detailed information:

```
Get-SCOMManagementGroup
```

Alert management

As an SCOM administrator, it is one of our day-to-day activities to monitor alerts and respond to them. One way to see all the alerts, thrown on the Operations Manager console is to log in and check for alerts and the other way is to use PowerShell to list all the alerts on the PowerShell console, which can be exported to an external file for later use. PowerShell provides the `Get-SCOMAlert` cmdlet to list all the alerts registered with Operations Manager.

With no arguments specified, the alert will list all the alerts registered with Operations Manager. The following example demonstrates the usage of a cmdlet with no arguments:

```
Get-SCOMAlert
```

However, in real time, we will not usually be interested in listing all the alerts. Usually, we will apply some sort of filter to the alerts to narrow down the output according to our requirement. The following example demonstrates a few of the filtering methods:

```
Get-SCOMAlert –Name "*Exchange*"
```

The preceding cmdlet will list all the SCOM alerts that have the word Exchange in the alert name:

```
Get-SCOMAlert | Where-Object {$_.ResolutionState –ne 255}
```

This will list only the alerts with a resolution state not equal to 255. When an alert is generated, its resolution state is New. Operators can change the resolution state for a new alert to Closed or to a custom resolution state that an administrator has created for the management group. The ID for New is 0 and the ID for Closed is 255. You can assign custom resolution states with any value from 2 through 254.

The following example will show you how to list the alert related to a particular group:

```
$Group = Get-SCOMGroup -DisplayName "TestGroup1"

$Instance = $Group.GetRelatedMonitoringObjects('Recursive')

$Alerts =Get-SCOMAlert -instance $Instance -ResolutionState (2..254)
```

We can also get the history of any particular alert or the list of alerts using PowerShell. We can use the Get-SCOMAlertHistory cmdlet to get the alert history:

```
$Alert = Get-SCOMAlert -Name "*Exchange*"

Get-SCOMAlertHistory -AlertName $Alert
```

Alert resolution

Once the issues are resolved, we are required to close the alert for tracking. As we are aware, there will be two kinds of alerts in SCOM—auto closure and manual closure alerts. Auto closure alerts will get closed when the SCOM detects that the issue is resolved in the agent. The alert will be auto moved to the closed alert tab.

In case of manual closure alerts, we are manually required to close the alerts when the issue is resolved or when the engineer resolves the ticket. The engineer has to manually set the status of alert to resolved.

We can use the Get-SCOMAlertResolutionState cmdlet to get the list of the alert resolution states already available in the database.

With no arguments specified, the cmdlet will list all the available resolution states. We can also specify the resolution state code as a parameter of the cmdlet to get the details of a particular resolution state:

```
Get-SCOMAlertResolutionState

Get-SCOMAlertResolutionState -ResolutionStateCode 10
```

PowerShell provides the Add-SCOMAlertResolutionState cmdlet to set the custom resolution state of the existing alert. We are required to provide a name for the new resolution state and the resolution state code as arguments to the cmdlet. The following example will add a new resolution state, Investigating, with the resolution state code as 20:

```
Add-SCOMAlertResolutionState -Name "Investigating" -ResolutionstateCode
20
```

Authoring

This topic involves the management of object discovery, reading and creating a new monitoring class, and reading and creating new groups.

Discovery management

Once the management pack is imported on the Operations Manger console, the next step is to enable discovery of objects on any particular group:

```
Get-SCOMDiscovery
```

PowerShell also allows us to disable the discovery of objects for any management pack. We can use the `Disable-SCOMDiscovery` cmdlet to disable the discovery of objects. Once the discovery is disabled, Operations Manager will stop monitoring the object with the rules and monitors defined in the management pack.

The following example will illustrate the usage of PowerShell to disable the discovery of the management pack. First, we are required to get the management pack for which we want to disable the discovery and class details. Then, we will use the `Disable-SCOMDiscovery` cmdlet to disable the discovery of objects:

```
$MP = Get-SCOMManagementPack -Name "Test.Guru.Com"

$Class = Get-SCOMClass -Name "Test Class"

$Discovery = Get-SCOMDiscovery -Name "MyDiscovery"

Disable-SCOMDiscovery -Class $Class -Discovery $Discovery -ManagementPack
$MP
```

The preceding code reads the management pack by the `"Test.Guru.Com"` name. It also gets the class name by the `"test class"` name and the discovery by the `"MyDiscovery"` name. It will disable the SCOM discovery by the `"MyDisovery"` name on the `"Test Class"` class with the `"Test.Guru.Com"` management pack name.

Class and instance

Class in Operations Manager represents the type of an object. All the instances of a class share the similar set of properties. We can get the list of classes in Operations Manager using the `Get-SCOMClass` cmdlet. With no parameter specified, the cmdlet will list all the available classes. We can also pass the name of the class as an argument to the cmdlet to get the details of that particular class. The following example demonstrates the usage of the `Get-SCOMClass` cmdlet both with and without the parameters:

```
Get-SCOMClass
```

```
Get-SCOMClass -Name "Test,Guru.FolderMonitor.Class1"
```

Every object in a class is considered as an instance of that class. All instances of a class share a similar set of properties. PowerShell provides a way to list all the instances of a class using the `Get-SCOMClassInstance` cmdlet. The following example demonstrates the usage of this cmdlet:

```
$Class = Get-SCOMClass -Name "Test.Guru.Foldermonitor.Class1"
```

```
Get-SCOMClassInstance -Class $Class
```

Groups

In Operations Manager, groups are used to hold the list of the managed objects. We can configure the group to be static or dynamic. PowerShell provides a way to list all the available groups in Operations Manager. We can use `Get-SCOMGroup` to list all the groups available in Operations Manager. With no parameters specified, the cmdlet will list all the available groups. We can pass the name of the group as a parameter to the cmdlet to get detailed information of that particular group. The following example will demonstrate the usage of the cmdlet:

```
Get-SCOMGroup
```

```
Get-SCOMGroup -DisplayName "TestGroup1"
```

Administration

This section deals with the management of core Operations Manager activities, such as creating management packs, subscriptions, agent-managed and agentless-managed entities, and many more.

Management servers

The management server is the main part of the Operations Manager architecture. It helps the administrator to configure and administrate the Operations Manager environment. It communicates with the agents and databases in the Operations Manager environment.

Each management group will have multiple management servers for high availability and load balance. A combination of multiple management servers will form a resource pool. When any management server resource pool fails, other management servers pick up the load to provide continuous service.

We can get the properties of any management server in the Operations Manager environment using the `Get-SCOMManagementServer` cmdlet. We are required to provide the name of the server as the parameter to the cmdlet:

```
Get-SCOMManagementServer -Name "Server01.guru.com"
```

Also, PowerShell facilitates the gathering of information of any gateway management servers. The gateway management server helps management servers across non-trusted domains. We can use the `Get-SCOMGatewayManagementServer` cmdlet to get the details of the gateway management servers in the environment:

```
Get-SCOMGatewayManagementServer -ComputerName "Server2.guru.com"
```

We can also get the list of all the gateway servers in the Operations Manager environment using wild characters (wildcards) in the computer name parameter:

```
Get-SCOMGatewayManagementServer -Name "*.guru.com"
```

Agent management

Like Configuration Manager, before we monitor any computer from Operations Manager, we are required to install an agent on the machine. The agent will collect information from the client, receive management pack monitoring rules from the management server, and act accordingly.

We can either manage computers through an agent or we can go for agentless monitoring. We can enable any near agent to act as a proxy agent, which will collect information from the agentless computer.

Agents will collect data from the computer and compare the sample with the predefined values in SCOM rules or SCOM monitors. Later, depending on the values, they will generate alerts on the Operations Manager console.

We can see the list of agent-managed computers either from the console or we can use PowerShell cmdlets to list all the computer names. PowerShell provides the `Get-SCOMAgent` cmdlet to list all the agent-managed computers in Operations Manager.

With no parameters specified, the cmdlet will list all the agent-managed computers from the environment. We can refine the output of any particular management server by passing the management server as a parameter to the cmdlet:

```
$MgmtServer = Get-SCOMManagementServer "MgmtServer1.guru.com"
Get-SCOMAgent -ManagementServer $MgmtServer
```

We can also get all the agent-managed computers in the `guru.com` domain using wild characters (wildcards) in the DNS hostname parameter. The following cmdlet will list all the agent-managed computers in the `guru.com` domain:

```
Get-SCOMAgent -DNSHostName "*.guru.com"
```

Agent installation

There are many ways in which we can install agents on computers:

- We can use group policies and deploy agents on the required computers
- We can also use the Configuration Manager software distribution method to push the agent software on the computer
- We can also make the agent a part of the operating system image that will get deployed during the deployment of the operating system

Apart from all the preceding methods, we can also manually install the agent using Command Prompt or PowerShell. PowerShell provides the `Install-SCOMAgent` cmdlet to install the SCOM agent on the target computer.

At a minimum, we are required to provide the name of the computer and the primary management server name as parameters to the cmdlet. The following example will illustrate the installation of an SCOM agent on a computer by passing the required parameters:

```
$PrimMgmtServer = Get-SCOMManagementServer -ComputerName
"SCOMMgmtServer1.Guru.com"

Install-SCOMAgent -DNSHostName "Client1.guru.com" -
PrimaryManagementServer $PrimMgmtServer
```

In addition to the primary management server and computer name, we can also specify the installation account and client action account (the client action account is used to gather information and run remediation actions on the client) as parameters to the cmdlet. We can use the `Get-Credential` cmdlet for an installation account to specify the installation account credentials during runtime.

When we see an SCOM agent malfunctioning, one of the basic troubleshooting steps that we follow is to repair the client agent. PowerShell provides the `Repair-SCOMAgent` cmdlet to repair the agent installed on a computer. The cmdlet will accept the name of the computer on which the agent is to be repaired as a parameter to the cmdlet:

```
Get-SCOMAgent -DNSHostName "Client1.guru.com" | Repair-SCOMAgent
```

This cmdlet will get the SOCM agent installed on the `"Client1.guru.com"` computer and repair the agent on the computer.

We can also uninstall the agent on the computer using the `Uninstall-SCOMAgent` cmdlet. This parameter will accept the name of the computer on which the agent is to be uninstalled as a parameter. We can also specify the action account as a parameter to the cmdlet:

```
$Computer = Get-SCOMAgent -DNSHostName "Client1.guru.com"

Uninstall-SCOMAgent -Agent $Computer
```

SCOM proxy agents

As discussed earlier, we can also make an agent act as a proxy agent. A proxy agent can be used for agentless monitoring of objects. PowerShell provides the `Enable-SCOMAgentProxy` cmdlet to enable any agent as a proxy agent, which can facilitate agentless monitoring of the objects.

We can pass a single computer or an array of computers as parameters to this cmdlet. In case of multiple computers, the cmdlet will enable proxy monitoring on the computer:

```
$SCOMAgent = Get-SCOMAgent -DNSHostName "Client1.guru.com"

Enable-SCOMAgentProxy $SCOMAgent -PassThru
```

Similarly, we can disable a proxy agent using PowerShell. PowerShell provides the `Disable-SCOMAgentProxy` cmdlet to disable a proxy on the required SCOM agent:

```
$SCOMAgent = Get-SCOMAgent -DNSHostName "Client1.guru.com"

Disable-SCOMAgentProxy $SCOMAgent
```

When we manually install the agent on a computer, we are required to manually approve the agent to enable monitoring and to communicate with the management server. Unless the agent is approved, the agent software cannot communicate with the management server and no monitoring can be performed.

We can use the `Get-SCOMPendingManagement` cmdlet to get the list of agents with the agent pending action type as manual approve. Then, we can approve the list using the `Approve-SCOMPendingManagement` cmdlet:

```
Get-SCOMPendingManagement | Where-Object {$_.AgentPendingActionType -eq
"ManualApproval"} | Approve-SCOMPendingManagement
```

This will get all the agents that are pending for manual approval and approve the list. We can also specify the action account and credentials as parameters to the cmdlet.

As an administrator, for any reason, if you want to deny any agent in the pending list to block communication with the management server, PowerShell provides the `Deny-SCOMPendingManagement` cmdlet to deny the agent from being monitored:

```
Get-SCOMPendingManagement | Where-Object {$_.AgentPendingActionType -eq
"ManualApproval"} | Deny-SCOMPendingManagement
```

This will get all the agents that are pending for manual approval and deny the list. We can also specify the action account and credentials as parameters to the cmdlet.

Management pack details

Being an Operations Manager administrator, we are well aware that management packs are the heart and soul of monitoring activities. Management packs typically contain monitoring settings for applications and services. Once the management pack is imported to the Configuration Manager console, it will discover the configured objects, and upon enabling the monitoring, it will start monitoring the objects configured for the same.

Management packs may contain rules, monitors, tasks, reports, and views. It depends on the monitoring requirements to design the management packs accordingly. Requirements may be as simple as monitoring a service or an event log, or it may be any custom complex requirement. Usually, in real-time scenarios, we follow script-based monitoring for any custom complex monitoring. We can use the VB or PowerShell scripting for this purpose.

PowerShell provides the `Get-SCOMManagementPack` cmdlet to list all the management packs available in the Operations Manager database. Without the specified parameters, the cmdlet will list all of the available management packs in the database. We can also specify the name of the management pack as the parameter to the cmdlet to list the properties of our interested management pack:

```
Get-SCOMManagementPack

Get-SCOMManagementPack -Name "Test.Guru.Folder.Monitor"
```

We can use the `Import-SCOMManagementPack` cmdlet to import any management packs on the SCOM database. Before you import any management packs, Operations Manager will validate the correctness of the management pack file, which will be either sealed (`.mp` extension) or unsealed (`.xml` extension).

 If you are planning to refer to the management packs as a reference management pack to some other management pack, it is always required that you seal the management pack before you import it to the Operations Manager console.

At a minimum, we are required to provide the full path of the management pack to be imported as a parameter to the cmdlet. Optionally, we can also specify the name of the management pack we will import. The following example will illustrate the import of a management pack:

```
Import-SCOMManagementPack -FullName "C:\SCOM\MP\Test.Guru.FolderMonitor.
mp"
```

Similarly, we can also export all the management packs available in the Operations Manager database as part of the maintenance activities using the `Export-SCOMManagementPack` cmdlet. At a minimum, this cmdlet will accept the path where the management packs are to be exported as parameters. With no parameters specified, the cmdlet will export all the management packs. We can use the `Get-SCOMManagementPack` cmdlet with the name of the required management pack, which pipelines to the `Export-SCOMManagementPack` cmdlet to export only the interested management packs. The following example will illustrate the usage of the `Export-SCOMManagementPack` cmdlet:

```
Get-SCOMManagementPack -Name "Test.Guru.FolderMonitor" |Export-
SCOMManagementPack -Path "C:\SCOM\MP\Archive"
```

We can also remove the unnecessary management packs for the Operations Manager database using the `Remove-SCOMManagementPack` cmdlet. It is always a good practice to remove all the unwanted management packs for the production environment when they are not in use. To remove a management pack for the console, we are required to provide the name of the management pack to be removed as a parameter to the cmdlet:

```
Remove-SCOMManagementPack -ManagementPack "Test.Guru.FolderMonitor"
```

You can also use an intermediate variable to hold the name of the management pack to be deleted:

```
$MP = Get-SCOMManagementPack | Where-object {$_.Name -eq "Test.Guru.
FolderMonitor"}
```

```
Remove-SCOMManagementPack -ManagementPack $MP
```

SCOM rules

SCOM rules are used to collect data from different sources, such as an event log, log files, and so on, and store that data in the database. SCOM rules will duplicate data to both the operational database and data warehouse. We usually target classes for rules and not groups.

Rules are event-driven and are mainly used for reporting, such as getting the availability report and performance report. Rules are also used when there is no good or bad condition to be considered. Rules will generate an alert when the event occurs and will not auto close. Alerts generated by rules are manually closed alerts.

PowerShell provides the `Get-SCOMRule` cmdlet to get all the rules in the Operations Manager database. To make the output more meaningful, we generally will give the name of the rule or rule pattern to narrow down the output according to our requirement:

```
Get-SCOMRule -Name "*FileMonitor*"
```

This cmdlet will retrieve all the SOCM rules that have `FileMonitor` in it. Similarly, we can use different wild character patterns to get the required output.

We can also use the `Get-SCOMManagementPack` cmdlet pipelines with the `Get-SCOMrule` cmdlet to list all the rules that are configured in a particular management pack:

```
Get-SCOMManagementPack -Name "Test.Guru.FolderMonitor" | Get-SCOMRule
```

The preceding cmdlet will first search for the management pack by the `"Test.Guru.FolderMonitor"` name and it will list down all the rules that are configured in the management pack.

As discussed before, SCOM rules target a class rather than group name. We can also get the list of all the SCOM rules targeted on a particular class. The following cmdlet will retrieve all the SCOM rules targeted on the class with the name `"TestClass"`:

```
Get-SCOMRule -Target (Get-SCOMClass -DisplayName "TestClass")
```

We can also directly specify the name or ID of the SCOM rule if we know how to get the complete details of that particular SCOM rule. We can either specify the name or ID of the SCOM rule as a parameter:

```
Get-SCOMRule -ID "XXXX-XXXXX-XXXXX-XXXXX"
Exampple: Get-SCOMRule -ID "6a5b9728-52de-9da2-c74c-1189582a91e5"
```

When we create any SCOM rule, the first thing we do is we enable the rule of any override management pack. We can enable any SCOM rule on a particular override. We can use the class name or the management pack name as the parameter to the cmdlet:

```
$Class = Get-SCOMClass -DisplayName "TestClass"
$Rule = Get-SCOMRule -DisplayName "TestRule"
$MP = Get-SCOMManagementPack -DisplayName "TestMP"
Enable-SCOMRule -Class $Class -Rule $Rule -managementPack $MP -Enforce
```

We can use `Disable-SCOMRule` to disable the existing SCOM rule and save to an override. We are required to provide the name of the management pack or the name of the class as the parameter to the cmdlet:

```
$Class = Get-SCOMClass -DisplayName "TestClass"

$Rule = Get-SCOMRule -DisplayName "TestRule"

$MP = Get-SCOMManagementPack -DisplayName "TestMP"

Disable-SCOMRule -Class $Class -Rule $Rule -managementPack $MP -Enforce
```

SCOM monitors

Like SCOM rules, management packs may also contain monitors. Monitors indicate the health of the managed objects. Alerts generated by monitors are called auto close alerts, which means that the alert generated by a monitor will be auto closed when the managed entity comes back to normal condition at any point of time. This defines a logic of how an SCOM agent can identify when something goes wrong with the managed objects.

SCOM provides three kinds of monitors:

- A unit monitor
- A dependency monitor
- An aggregate monitor

A unit monitor measures particular aspects of an application, such as the performance, watching registry, log files monitoring, running a script, and so on. A dependency monitor provides the health roll up between two classes and the aggregate monitor combines the health of multiple monitors.

PowerShell provides the `Get-SCOMMonitor` cmdlet to list all the available monitors of a particular management pack or the monitors of any particular class. We can specify the ID/name parameter to pass the ID/name of the monitor that we are interested in to get the complete details of it.

Here are a few examples of how to use the `Get-SCOMMonitor` cmdlet. First, we will see how to get the details of a particular monitor by passing the name of that monitor as a parameter. Here, `"Guru.Test.FolderMonitor.monitor"` is the name of the monitor I am interested in:

```
Get-SCOMMonitor -Name "Guru.Test.FolderMonitor.monitor"
```

We can also list all the available monitors in a particular management pack. The following example aims at listing all the monitors in the `"Guru.Test.FolderMonitor"` management pack:

```
Get-SCOMManagementPack -Name "Guru.Test.FolderMonitor" | Get-SCOMMonitor
```

We can also list all the available monitors that have a given class that is included by passing the class name as a parameter. The following example aims at listing all the monitors that have the `"Guru.Test.FolderMonitor.Class1"` class:

```
Get-SCOMMonitor -Instance (Get-SCOMClassInstance -DisplayName "Databases")
```

PowerShell provides us the means to enable or disable monitors. We can use `Enable-SCOMMonitor` to enable any SCOM monitor. We are required to provide the management pack name and the class name as parameters to the cmdlet.

The following example demonstrates the usage of the `Enable-SCOMMonitor` cmdlet. The example aims at enabling the `"Guru.Test.FolderMonitor.Monitor"` monitor of the `"Guru.Test.Monitor"` management pack on the `"Guru.Test.Foldermonitor.Class1"` class:

```
$MP = Get-SCOMManagementPack -Name "Guru.Test.Foldermonitor"

$Class = Get-SCOMClass -Name "Guru.Test.Foldermonitor.Class1"

$Monitor = Get-SCOMMonitor -Name "Guru.Test.FolderMonitor.Monitor"

Enable-SCOMMonitor -Class $Class -ManagementPack $MP -Monitor $Monitor
```

PowerShell also provides the `Disable-SCOMMonitor` cmdlet to disable unused monitors if any. The cmdlet requires the name of the monitor, management pack name, and target class as parameters to the cmdlet. The logic works similar to how `Enable-SCOMMonitor` works.

The following example demonstrates the usage of the `Disable-SCOMMonitor` cmdlet. It aims at enabling the `"Guru.Test.FolderMonitor.Monitor"` monitor of the `"Guru.Test.Monitor"` management pack on the `"Guru.Test.Foldermonitor.Class1"` class:

```
$MP = Get-SCOMManagementPack -Name "Guru.Test.Foldermonitor"

$Class = Get-SCOMClass -Name "Guru.Test.Foldermonitor.Class1"

$Monitor = Get-SCOMMonitor -Name "Guru.Test.FolderMonitor.Monitor"

Disable-SCOMMonitor -Class $Class -ManagementPack $MP -Monitor $Monitor
```

Database grooming

Database grooming is one of the standard maintenance activities of Operations Manager. Database grooming will delete all the unnecessary data from the Operations Manager database. PowerShell provides the `Get-SCOMDatabaseGroomingSetting` cmdlet to see the available settings in Operations Manager. With no parameters specified, the cmdlet will provide the settings configured on Operations Manager:

```
Get-SCOMDatabaseGroomingSetting
```

PowerShell also provides the `Set-SCOMDatabaseGroomingSetting` cmdlet to modify any changes to the database grooming settings. The following example sets the alert retention period of the operational database. The following cmdlet will also set the availability data retention period along with the event data retention period. For all the configurations, the value is set to 5 in the following example:

```
Set-SCOMDatabaseGroomingSetting –AlertDaysToKeep 5 –
AvailabilityHistoryDaysToKeep 5 –EventDaysToKeep 5
```

Alert notifications

For best utilization of SCOM monitoring and to help administrators take quick action on the alerts, Microsoft has provided a notification mechanism as a feature in SCOM. Whenever there is an alert from any particular monitor or from any particular class, configurations in SCOM can be set so that a notification will be sent to the administrator in the form of an e-mail or an instant message or via a short message service.

PowerShell provides the `Get-SCOMNotificationChannel` cmdlet to get the list of available notification channels for a management group. With no parameters specified, the cmdlet will retrieve the list of the available notification channels in the management group. We can also specify the name of the notification channel as a parameter to the cmdlet to get more information of that particular notification channel. The following example demonstrates the usage of the cmdlet with and without parameters:

```
Get-SCOMNotificationChannel
```

```
Get-SCOMNotificationChannel –Displayname "Email Channel"
```

We can add our own custom notification channels as and when required. PowerShell provides the `Add-SCOMNotificationChannel` cmdlet to add new notification channels to the existing list. To deliver notifications, a notification channel uses a delivery mechanism, such as an e-mail, instant messenger, a short message service, or command.

The following example demonstrates the creation of the SMTP e-mail notification channel. For the e-mail notification channel, first, we are required to create a subject and the body of the e-mail to be sent. The body and subject formatting of the e-mail looks a bit tricky, but this remains standard across:

```
$Sub = "SCOM Alert: `$Data[Default='Not Present']/Context/DataItem/
AlertName`$"

$Body = "Owner: `$Data[Default='Not Present']/Context/DataItem/
AlertOwner`$"

Add-SCOMNotificationChannel -Name "Guru.Test" -Server "mail.guru.com"
-From "scomadmin@guru.net" -Subject $Sub -Body $Body
```

We can also remove any of the existing notification channels for the list whenever required. PowerShell provides the `Remove-SCOMNotificationChannel` cmdlet to remove notification channels from the list. We can use the name of the notification channel as a parameter to the cmdlet that specifies the name of the notification channel to be deleted for the existing list. The following example demonstrates the deletion of the notification channel using the `Remove-SCOMNotificationChannel` cmdlet:

```
$NC = Get-SCOMNotificationChannel –DisplayName "TestNotificationChannel"

Remove-SCOMNotificationChannel –Action $NC
```

Using PowerShell, we can also list the registered subscribers for alert notification. PowerShell provides the `Get-SCOMNotificationSubscriber` cmdlet to list all the registered subscribers. With no parameters specified, the cmdlet will list all the available subscribers. We can specify any subscriber name as a parameter to the cmdlet to get detailed information of any specific subscriber:

```
Get-SCOMNotificationSubscriber

Get-SCOMNotificationSubscriber –Name "TestUser1"
```

We can also add the new subscribers using PowerShell, just like the way we did from the console. We can use the `Add-SCOMNotificationSubscriber` cmdlet to add new subscribers to the list. The following example shows how to add a new subscriber to the list:

```
Add-SCOMNotificationSubscriber –Name "TestUser2" –DeviceList "TestUser2@
guru.com"
```

Similarly, we can remove any listed subscriber via PowerShell using the `Remove-SCOMNotificationSubscriber` cmdlet. We are required to provide the name of the subscriber to be removed as a parameter to the cmdlet. The following example demonstrates the removal of a subscriber from the list:

```
$User = Get-SCOMNotificationSubscriber –Name "TestUser1"

Remove-SCOMNotificationSubscriber  -Name $User
```

Summary

By now, you should be able to understand the basic cmdlet to manage Operations Manager. You should be comfortable in using simple cmdlets to read and update simple SCOM configurations. In the next chapter, we will see the more advanced usage of cmdlets to configure and manage Operations Manager.

5
Scenario-based Scripting for SCOM Administration

The last chapter provided a basic understanding of how to manage **System Center Operations Manager** (**SCOM**) operations through PowerShell. Now, it's time to look at some of the real-time scenarios that will give us a better understanding of how to use PowerShell to carry out some of the day-to-day SCOM activities. Here, we are trying to cover most of the common scenarios that we, as administrators, would need to perform on a daily basis. We can still do much more than what is covered in this chapter.

 The code blocks demonstrated in this chapter will not include error-handling mechanisms. When using code in real-time scenarios, it is very important to include error-handling mechanisms to avoid errors.

For a better understanding of the following code blocks, you can try them out in your lab environment and analyze the output. Try to modify the output according to your requirements. This will give you the confidence to write and implement your code in the production environment.

Before implementing any code block in production, make sure that you have thoroughly tested the code in the development or test environment. Once you have satisfactorily tested the code in the development environment, move the code to the pre-production environment, and test for its truthiness. Once you are very sure that the script is working perfectly and delivering expected results, implement it in the production environment.

There are a few basic things that you should know before you start scripting the scenarios. One of them is the resolution state and the code associated with the state. The following table lists the alert state and the corresponding code for that state:

State	Code
New	0
Closed	255

Also, it is equally important to be aware of the alert severity and its corresponding code. The following table maps the alert severity with its corresponding code:

Alert severity	Code
Information	0
Warning	1
Critical	2

With the assumption that you are familiar and comfortable with the basic exercises that we discussed in the last chapter, let us now consider some real-time scenarios, and how to automate those scenarios using PowerShell.

This chapter covers the following topics:

- Resolving all SCOM alerts
- Listing and exporting all SCOM monitors
- Listing and exporting all SCOM overrides
- Listing and exporting gray agents in SCOM
- Finding management pack details for a particular alert
- Listing past alerts
- Backing up unsealed management packs
- Counting alerts created by a monitor
- Enabling specific SCOM monitors
- Listing all updated management packs
- Listing and exporting repeating SCOM alerts
- Getting SCOM alerts specific to a computer
- Listing all unhealthy SCOM agents
- Disabling SCOM alerts
- Listing all heartbeat failure machines

- Listing all management server open alerts
- Listing management servers in maintenance mode
- Listing health status of management servers
- Putting an IIS 7 application pool in maintenance mode

Resolving all SCOM alerts

This example demonstrates how an SCOM administrator can resolve all the alerts that are older than five days. We can use the same example code to resolve all the alerts that are older than our custom required date by changing the value from 5 to our custom requirement as shown in the following example:

```
$targetDate = (Get-Date).AddDays(-5)

$allAlerts = Get-SCOMAlert


$filterAlerts = $allAlerts | Where-Object {($_.ResolutionState -eq 0)
  -and ($_.LastModified -lt $targetDate) -and ($_.IsMonitorAlert -eq
  $false)}


$filterAlerts | Resolve-SCOMAlert
```

Listing and exporting all SCOM monitors

This example demonstrates how to list and export all the available monitors in the specific management pack.

Assumptions

In the following example, we will extract all the monitors of the `FileMonitor.Guru.Test.MP` custom management pack and store it in `C:\SCOM\MP\MP.txt`:

```
$MP = "FileMonitor.Guru.Test.MP"

$FileLocation = "C:\SCOM\MP\MP.txt"

$monitorList = Get-Monitor -ManagementPack $mp
```

Listing and exporting all SCOM overrides

The following example demonstrates how to list and export all the overrides for a specific management pack using PowerShell. The same example can be used to list overrides for any other management packs.

Assumptions

In the following example, we will list overrides for the `FileMonitor.Guru.Test.MP` management pack. You can replace the value with your required management pack name:

```
$fileLocation = "C:\SCOM\MP\Overrides.txt"
$mp = Get-SCOMManagementPack -DisplayName "File Monitor MP"
$overrides = $mp.GetOverrides()
$overrides | Out-File $fileLocation
```

Listing and exporting gray agents in SCOM

SCOM administrators need to list and troubleshoot gray agents in SCOM. You can access the Microsoft TechNet link `https://technet.microsoft.com/en-in/library/hh212723.aspx` for more details on gray agents. Here is a test code that will list all the gray agents and export the results in a text file. We can use this file as a reference for further troubleshooting or we can automate the troubleshooting process by feeding this file as an input to other code that will carry on the troubleshooting activities:

```
$class = Get-SCOMClass -Name "Microsoft.SystemCenter.Agent"
$mObject = $class | Get-SCOMMonitoringObject | Where-Object {
  $_.IsAvailable -eq $false}
$mObject | select DisplayName
```

Finding management pack details for a particular alert

This is one of the common requirements that both SCOM administrators and management pack developers will be interested in: the details of the management pack responsible for a particular alert.

Here, we are trying to get the details of the alert that has `File Transfer Error` in the name of the alert. We can use any wild characters of our choice to get the details of an alert for the management pack mapping we are interested in. Also, the code will fetch only the first alert with `File Transfer Error` in its name:

```
$alertName = "File Transfer Error"
$allAlerts = Get-SCOMAlert
```

```
$alert = $allAlerts | Where {$_.Name -like $alertName}
  | Select -First 1
If ($alert.IsMonitorAlert -eq "True")
{
  Write-Host "This is a monitor-generated alert"
  $monitor = Get-SCOMMonitor -ID $alert.MonitoringRuleID
  $mp = $monitor.GetManagementPack()
  $infoObj = New-Object PSObject -Property @{Enabled =
  $monitor.Enabled; DisplayName = $monitor.DisplayName;
  ManagementPack = $mp}
  $infoObj | Select Enabled, DisplayName, ManagementPack
}
else
{
  Write-Host "This is a rule-generated alert"
  $rule = Get-SCOMRule -ID $alert.MonitoringRuleID
  $rule | Select Enabled, DisplayName, ManagementPack
}
```

Listing past alerts

The following code will list all the alerts generated a day before you run the script. You can make it according to your custom date just by changing the value that we add to the date (-1 in the current example) in the following script:

```
$AllAlerts = Get-SCOMAlert
$AlertDateYesterdayBegin = [DateTime]::Today.AddDays(-1)
  $AlertDateYesterdayEnd = [DateTime]::Today.AddDays
  (-1).AddSeconds(86399)


$YesterdayAlerts = @($AllAlertsW | where {$_.
  TimeRaised -ge $AlertDateYesterdayBegin
  -and $_.TimeRaised -lt $AlertDateYesterdayEnd})


$YesterdayAlerts
```

Backing up unsealed management packs

As SCOM administrators, we need to take backups of the unsealed management packs on a daily basis as part of the SCOM maintenance activities. We can use the TechNet link `https://technet.microsoft.com/en-in/library/hh212794.aspx` to get detailed information of the management pack, its parts, and types.

The following code demonstrates how to take a backup of all the unsealed management packs that use PowerShell:

```
$AllMPs = Get-SCOMManagementPack

$UnsealedMPs = $AllMPs | where {$_.Sealed -eq $false}

# Now $UnseledMPs contains all unsealed MPs.
  Next is to export the contents of $UnSeledMPs

$UnseledMPsExport-SCOMmanagementpack -path C:\MPBackups
```

Counting alerts created by a monitor

The following code will demonstrate how to count the number of alerts created by the monitor over the last five days. This can be used for reporting. We can change the time interval just by changing the `-5` value in the following code. Also, this code will fetch only closed alerts (code `255`). We can change the following code as per the requirement:

```
$PastDate =

(Get-Date).Date.AddDays(-5)

$AllAlerts = Get-SCOMAlert

$AlertCount = ($AllAlerts -criteria 'ResolutionState = "255"
  AND IsMonitorAlert = "True"| Where-Object {$_.
  LastModified -gt $PastDate }).count

$AlertCount
```

Enabling specific SCOM monitors

This code demonstrates how to enable a specific monitor from a specific management pack. As we are aware, even after we import a new management pack with several monitors configured, it will not be effective until we enable the monitor. So, here is the sample code that will help you to enable the monitor through PowerShell.

Here, we will enable the `TestClass.FileMonitor.TestMP.Monitor` monitor in the `FileMonitor.TestMP.MP` management pack on the `TestClass.FileMonitor.TestMP.CLS1` class:

```
$MP = Get-SCOMManagementPack -displayname
  "FileMonitor.TestMP.MP" | where {$_.Sealed -eq $False}

$Class = Get-SCOMClass -DisplayName
  "TestClass.FileMonitor.TestMP.CLS1"

$Monitor = Get-SCOMMonitor -DisplayName
  "TestClass.FileMonitor.TestMP.Monitor"

Enable-SCOMMonitor -Class $Class -ManagementPack
  $MP -Monitor $Monitor
```

Listing all updated management packs

The code here will get the list of all management packs updated in the last 24 hours. We can change this interval by changing the hours (24 in this example) in the following code to get the list of the management packs updated in the custom intervals:

```
$MyDate = (Get-Date).AddHours(-24)

$AllMPs = Get-SCOMManagementPack

$ModifiedMPs= $AllMPs | Where {$_.LastModified -gt $MyDate}
  | Select-Object Name, LastModified | Sort LastModified

$ModifiedMPs | Out-File -FilePath "C:\SCOM\MP\updated.txt"
```

Listing and exporting repeating SCOM alerts

As an SCOM administrator, you will be asked to provide a list of the top repeating alerts. The following example lists and exports the top 20 repeating alerts to a text file. We can change the count of 20 to a custom number by just changing the count in the following code:

```
$AllAlerts = Get-SCOMAlert

$RepeatAlert = $AllAlerts | Sort -desc RepeatCount
  | Select-Object -First 20 Name, RepeatCount,
  MonitoringObjectPath, Description

$RepeatAlert | Out-File -FilePath "C:\SCOM\MP\RepeatAlerts.txt"
```

Getting SCOM alerts specific to a computer

This code demonstrates how to get the alert list specific to a computer. We can change the value of `$ComputerName` to list alerts from specific computer.

The following example lists the alerts generated from the `Test Computer` machine:

```
$ComputerName = "TestComputer"

$AllAlerts = Get-SCOMAlert

$MyAlerts = $AllAlerts -criteria
  "NetbiosComputerName = '$ComputerName'"
  | export-csv c:\alert.csv
```

Listing all unhealthy SCOM agents

The following code lists all the SCOM agents that are not healthy for various reasons. We can use this report as a reference for further troubleshooting:

```
$AllAgents = Get-SCOMAgent

$UnHealthyAgents = $AllAgents | where
  {$_.HealthState -ne "Success"} | select Name,HealthState

Write-Host "Unhealthy Agent list = `n $UnHealthyAgents"
```

Disabling SCOM alerts

This example demonstrates how to disable multiple rules matching a certain criteria from a particular management pack. One of the criteria selected here is to delete all the rules that match the rule name.

Here, we are trying to delete all the rules containing `FileCount` in the name from the `TestFile.TestMP.MP` management pack. You can change the values according to your requirements:

```
$MP = Get-SCOMManagementPack -Displayname "TestFile.TestMP.MP" | `

where {$_.Sealed -eq $False}

$Class = Get-SCOMClass -Name "TestClass1.TestMP"

$Rule = Get-SCOMRule -DisplayName "*FileCount*"

Disable-SCOMRule -Class $Class -Rule $Rule -ManagementPack
  $MP -Enforce
```

Listing all heartbeat failure machines

Heartbeat failure is one the most important alerts that should be prioritized and handled. The following code will get you the top 20 machines that are experiencing frequent heartbeat failure issues:

```
$HBAlerts = Get-SCOMAlert -Name "Health Service Heartbeat*"

$AlertList = $HBAlerts | select Name, `

MonitoringObjectDisplayName | Group-Object -Property
  MonitoringObjectDisplayName `| sort-object -Property Count
  -descending | select -first 20 count, name
```

Listing all management server open alerts

One of the common requirements for the daily SCOM health check report is to list the alerts related to management servers. The following PowerShell code lists all the management server open alerts:

```
$ManagementServers = Get-SCOMManagementServer

$AlertDetails = @()

foreach ($ManagementServer in $ManagementServers)

{

$AlertDetails += get-SCOMAlert -Criteria ("NetbiosComputerName = '"
  +    $ManagementServer.ComputerName + "'") | where
  {$_.ResolutionState -ne '255' -and $_.
  MonitoringObjectFullName -Match 'Microsoft.SystemCenter'} |
  select TimeRaised,Name,Description,Severity

}


$AlertDetails
```

Listing management servers in the maintenance mode

It is always an important daily health check requirement to list all the management servers in the maintenance mode. The following code lists all the SCOM management servers in the maintenance mode. This code will simply print whether the management server is in the maintenance mode or not. We can alter it to make the output a part of any particular report:

```
$MSs = get-SCOMGroup -DisplayName "Operations Manager
  Management Servers" | Get-SCOMClassInstance
foreach ($MS in $MSs)
{
  if($MS.inMaintenanceMode -eq "False")
  {
      Write-Host $MS.DisplayName, "is not in Maintenance Mode"
  }
  Else
  {
      Write-Host $MS.DisplayName, "is in Maintenance Mode"
  }
}
```

Listing the health status of management servers

The following code demonstrates how to get the health status of management servers. The code will read the status of all management servers in the environment and display the status message. In an environment where all the management servers are healthy, the code will write a generic message that all the management servers are healthy. We can also generate the output in the form of a report:

```
$MSUnhealthCount = Get-SCOMManagementServer |
  where {$_.HealthState -ne "Success"} | Measure-Object
if($MSUnhealthCount .Count -gt 0)
{
```

```
$UnHealthyMS = Get-SCOMManagementServer | where
{$_.HealthState -ne "Success"} | select
DisplayName,HealthState,IsGateway

$UnHealthyMS
}
Else
{
  Write-Host "All management servers are in healthy state"
}
```

Putting an IIS 7 application in the maintenance mode

The following example demonstrates how to put an IIS 7 application in maintenance mode. This can be used as a generic example to put any other required application in the maintenance mode:

```
$ MonitoringClass = get-SCOMclass | where-object {$_.Name -eq
  "Microsoft.Windows.InternetInformationServices.ApplicationPool"}


$objPool1 = get-scomclassinstance -Class  $Monitoringclass |
  where-object {($_.Path -match "webserver.domain.com")
  -and ($_.DisplayName -match "AppPoolName")}
  $CurrentTime = [DateTime]::Now


Start-SCOMMaintenanceMode -instance $objPool1 -endtime
  $CurrentTime.addHours(0.2) -reason "PlannedOther"
  -comment "Test of MM for AppPool"
```

In the preceding example, the IIS 7 application pool will be in the maintenance mode for 0.2 hours with the reason as PlannedOther, and Test of MM for AppPool as comments, all of which can be changed as per the requirements.

Summary

This chapter gave you an in-depth idea of how to use PowerShell with SCOM to perform various day-to-day activities. This should give administrators confidence to use PowerShell for their normal tasks. In this chapter, you saw how to use PowerShell scripts to get the work done easily in various scenarios without any human errors. During the first read, the code may look complex, but regular practice can ease the learning.

The easy way to start learning PowerShell with SCOM is to start using it. Try using the PowerShell cmdlets whenever possible, instead of going for the GUI methods. This covers most of the day-to-day activities we use on the SCOM console. Automating the regular tasks will always help to reduce time and human error.

6
Administration of Service Manager through PowerShell

In this chapter, we will focus on the third product of the System Center product family, that is, **Service Manager**. Service Manager is a platform to manage your IT services and automate the process involved in incident management for your organization. It also helps us to identify and adapt the best practices from **Microsoft Operations Framework** (**MOF**) and **Information Technology Infrastructure Library** (**ITIL**). It also provides support for change control and asset lifecycle management.

When it comes to the use of Service Manager with Windows PowerShell, it includes many PowerShell cmdlets that help you perform certain tasks without using the traditional Service Manager console. For example, you can use the `Import-SCSMManagementPack` cmdlet to import a management pack, and there are other similar commands as well. All the Service Manager cmdlets have the `SCSM` prefix to noun part.

The Service Manager cmdlets are available in two separate modules listed as follows:

- **Administrative cmdlets**: These cmdlets are available under the module named `System.Center.Service.Manager`. These cmdlets are basically used to perform common administrative tasks.

- **Data warehouse cmdlets**: These cmdlets are available under the module named `Microsoft.EnterpriseManagement.Warehouse.Cmdlets`. These cmdlets are basically used to operate SCSM data warehouse tasks.

By default, Windows PowerShell installs all the modules to the specified paths available at `$env:PSModulePath`, respectively. As a special case, Service Manager modules are not available in the default path. So, you won't be able to retrieve Service Manager modules by running the `Get-Module -List` cmdlet.

It is recommended that you use data warehouse cmdlets on the data warehouse database server, even though you can run them on both the Service Manager Management server and the Data Warehouse Management server.

The following procedures will help you get started with the Service Manager cmdlets.

To open a Service Manager Windows PowerShell session from the Service Manager console, perform the following steps:

1. In the **Service Manager** console, click on **Administration**.
2. On the **Tasks** pane, click on the **Start PowerShell** session.

The administrator cmdlet module is automatically preimported in this session. To open a Service Manager Windows PowerShell session from Windows, perform the following steps:

1. On the taskbar of the computer that hosts the Service Manager Management server, click on **Start**, point your cursor to **All Programs**, and then click on **Microsoft System Center**.
2. Click on **Service Manager 2012** and then click on **Service Manager Shell**.

The administrator cmdlet module is automatically preimported in this session. To list all the Service Manager cmdlets, perform the following steps:

1. Open a Service Manager Windows PowerShell session.
2. To list the cmdlets that are included in the administrator module, in the Service Manager Windows PowerShell session, type the following command statement in the console and then press *Enter*:

    ```
    Get-Command -Module System.Center.Service.Manager
    ```

3. To list the cmdlets that are included in the data warehouse module, in the Service Manager Windows PowerShell session, type the following command statement in the console and then press *Enter*:

    ```
    Get-Command -Module
        Microsoft.EnterpriseManagement.Warehouse.Cmdlets
    ```

To perform the same set of activities using the regular PowerShell console, perform the following steps.

For SCSM Management servers, enter the following command in the console:

```
Import-Module 'C:\Program Files\Microsoft System Center 2012\Service
    Manager\Powershell\System.Center.Service.Manager.psd1▯
```

For Data Warehouse Management servers, place the following command in the console:

```
Import-Module 'C:\Program Files\Microsoft System Center 2012\Service
  Manager\Microsoft.EnterpriseManagement.Warehouse.Cmdlets.psd1⊠
```

SMlets

Now that we have a basic understanding of how to import and get the details of Service Manager PowerShell cmdlets, let's move toward the application of these available cmdlets.

Before jumping to the functionality, we will get the details of the additional external cmdlets.

There are a few open source projects available that provide an extension to the functionality that a normal SCSM PowerShell console has. One such SMlets codeplex project is created by James Truher. By default, the System Center Integration pack for SCSM and Orchestrator doesn't have all the functionalities to perform full automation. This SMlets project allows you to get some extensive functions that get added to the existing functionality. The SMlets project can be found at http://smlets.codeplex.com.

The following is the information to get started with the basic use of SMlets.

The default **Service Manager 2012 integration pack** for Orchestrator has five actions that can be used to create objects. This is where SMlets come into play:

1. The first step is to download and install SMlets on your Orchestrator server.

2. Once you have SMlets installed properly, open up the PowerShell console on your Orchestrator server and initialize the SMlets by running:

   ```
   Import-Module SMlets
   ```

3. To formulate the tasks, we first need to define which classes or types of objects we will be dealing with later for Service Manager. We will mainly use the Get-SCSMClass and Get-SCSMEnumeration commands to set up the variable and required class objects. Here's how you can do this:

   ```
   $SMSRClass = Get-SCSMClass -Name
     System.WorkItem.ServiceRequest
   ```

   The preceding statement will load the System.WorkItem.ServiceRequest class object to the $SMSRClass variable.

   ```
   $SMSRPri = Get-SCSMEnumeration -Name
     ServiceRequestPriorityEnum.Medium
   ```

The preceding statement will help us to retrieve the priority of the `ServiceRequest` object defined in the earlier step:

```
$SMSRUrg = Get-SCSMEnumeration -Name
    ServiceRequestUrgencyEnum.Medium
```

The preceding statement will help us to define the urgency of the `ServiceRequest` object defined in the earlier step:

```
$SMSRArea = Get-SCSMEnumeration -Name
    ServiceRequestAreaEnum.Other
```

The preceding statement will help us to define the area of the `ServiceRequest` object defined in the earlier step:

```
$SMSRTitle = "Service Request Title"
```

The preceding statement will help us to specify the title of the `ServiceRequest` object defined in the earlier step. The title is an important item to identify a service request uniquely. We would recommend you to use a unique title value for each service request that is created.

4. The next step is to prepare the argument list that will be used to define the properties for an SCSM object to create a new service request. We prefer to use a hash or an array to make a list of arguments that are required at a later point in time. The arguments can be gathered using the following step:

```
$SMSRArgs = @{ Title = $SMSRTitle;
Urgency = $SMSRUrg; Priority = $SMSRPri;
ID = "SMSR{0}"; Area = $SMSRArea;
Description = "Service Request Description"}
```

The Key to Value mapping is pretty self-explanatory here; however, in the line where we are defining `ID` and `{0}`, we will make Service Manager auto-append a number and this will end up making our ID look like `SMSR1234`.

5. Now that we have all the basic information required for our service request, we can create it. SMlets do not have a `New-SCSMServiceRequest` cmdlet, so we need to use a more generic `New-SCSMObject` command. The following is the step to create a new service request:

```
New-SCSMObject -Class $SRSMClass -PropertyHashtable $SRSMArgs
```

The preceding command statement will use the service request class and service request arguments gathered in the earlier steps. This command will immediately create the service request.

The last thing that we can do for our service request is apply the necessary service request template to our request. We can use a command to get the service request we just created and the service request template that we wish to apply.

Incident reporting

One more exciting thing that we can do using the Service Manager cmdlets is incident reporting. We can create a simple report of open (active and pending) incidents in System Center Service Manager 2012 and this can be easily done using the SMlets discussed earlier. However, it is good to have the option for my report to be generated by a group of users on their own machines, so it was preferable to do this using the native SCSM 2012 cmdlets (which the users already have installed as part of the SCSM 2012 installation):

1. Import the SCSM Native cmdlets:

    ```
    Import-Module "C:\Program Files\Microsoft System Center
      2012\Service Manager\Powershell\
      System.Center.Service.Manager.psd1"
    ```

2. Get the name of your SCSM server:

    ```
    $MySCSMServer = "SCSM Server Name"

    New-SCSMManagementGroupConnection -ComputerName $MySCSMServer

     $objRelationshipAssignedToUser = Get-SCSMRelationship
      -Name "System.WorkItemAssignedToUser"

    $objRelationshipAffectedUser = Get-SCSMRelationship
      -Name "System.WorkItemAffectedUser"
    ```

3. Get an object that contains all the open incidents:

    ```
    $objIncidentsOpen = (Get-SCClassInstance -Class
      (Get-SCClass -Name "System.WorkItem.Incident"))
      | Where-Object {$_.Status.ToString() -ne
      "IncidentStatusEnum.Closed" -and $_.Status.ToString()
      -ne "IncidentStatusEnum.Resolved"}
    ```

4. Format the object with calculated properties to display the required information:

    ```
    $objIncidentsOpen | Select-Object Id, Title,
      @{Name="Source";Expression={$_.Source.DisplayName}},
      CreatedDate, Priority, @{Name="Affected User";
      Expression = {$_.GetRelatedObjectsWhereSource
      ($objRelationshipAffectedUser)}},
      @{Name="Status";Expression={$_.Status.DisplayName}},
      @{Name="SupportGroup";
      Expression={$_.TierQueue.DisplayName}},
      @{Name="Assigned To"; Expression =
      {$_.GetRelatedObjectsWhereSource
      ($objRelationshipAssignedToUser)}}
    ```

This script should work on any machine that has the PowerShell and SCSM console installed. The output consists of pure PowerShell objects and can be redirected to CSV or HTML files if required.

The purpose of having System Center Service Manager is to implement incident, change, and problem management and to reduce manual activities by automating them. The tool has a strong workflow that allows us to perform various activities, such as creating, closing, and updating tickets/changes/incidents.

There are many repetitive tasks for incident and change managers to perform on a daily basis and it is highly recommended that you automate them. The following are the two activities that are common for most of the environments:

- When the changes are completed, auto close those changes after a certain number of days

- When the incidents are resolved, auto close those incidents after a certain number of days

Auto closing the resolved incidents and closing the completed changes

To perform these operations, we will leverage the external module available as SMlet from CodePlex. We can perform the same using legacy modules, but SMlets have extensive functionalities already implemented that bring ease to our task automation. We need to download the SMlets installer from `http://smlets.codeplex.com/` on the Service Manager server along with the Service Manager authoring console from `http://www.microsoft.com/en-us/download/details.aspx?id=10639` for SCSM 2010, and `http://www.microsoft.com/en-us/download/details.aspx?id=28726` for SCSM 2012.

You can implement the following two `.ps1` files to auto close the completed changes and resolved incidents after a certain number of days. For example, in the following example, we are taking 7 days to auto close the changes and incidents. The number of days are dynamic and can be set differently for various environments by changing the `-168` part (168/24=7 days) in the script.

Close the resolved incidents after seven days of inactivity:

```
Import-Module SMlets

$DaysOld = (Get-Date).addhours(-168)

$IncidentsToClose = Get-SCSMObject -Class (Get-SCSMClass -Name
    System.WorkItem.Incident$) | where{$_.lastmodified -
    lt $DaysOld -AND $_.Status -like "*Resol*"};

$IncidentsToClose | Set-SCSMObject -property Status -Value Closed;
```

Close the completed changes after seven days of inactivity:

```
$DaysOld = (Get-Date).addhours(-168);

Import-Module SMlets;

$ChangeClass = Get-SCSMClass System.WorkItem.ChangeRequest$

$AllChanges = Get-SCSMObject -Class $ChangeClass

$ChangeToClose = $AllChanges | where {$_.lastmodified
    -lt $DaysOld -AND $_.Status -like "*Complet*"};

$ChangeToClose | Set-SCSMObject –property Status –Value Closed;
```

If you don't feel like setting up an SLA with Service Manager and checking the waiting time for the incident assignment, use this quick one liner command:

```
Get-SCSMClassInstance -Class (Get-SCSMClass -Name
    System.WorkItem.Incident) |  Where-Object {$_.
    ?FirstAssignedDate -eq $null } | select Title, ID,
    @{Name='Time';Expression = { (New-TimeSpan $_.CreatedDate).
    Hours}} | where {$_.Time -gt 0}
```

This will show all the incidents that don't have `FirstAssignedDate` then create a time span between the current time and `CreatedDate`, and selecting the ones where that time span (in hours) is more than zero-meaning one hour at least. This, of course, can be changed at will.

Just note that if it's over 24 hours, the `.Hours` value is going to be back at zero. So, either expand the criteria (to include days) or make sure you get those assigned.

Changing the status of a service request

If you need to change the status of a service request in Service Manager 2012, you can do this with PowerShell. The following is an example:

Before running the PowerShell commands, install SMlets and import the module in the PowerShell prompt by running the following line:

```
Import-Module SMLets
```

The next thing to do is to get the appropriate class so that we can create an object from it. Use the following line to capture the service request class:

```
$Class = Get-SCSMClass -Name System.WorkItem.ServiceRequest
```

Other classes that can be used based on the requirement are as follows:

```
System.workitem.ChangeRequest
System.workitem.Incident
System.workitem.Problem
System.workitem.ReleaseRecord
```

Now it is time to create a class object from the class that was captured in the previous step:

```
Get-SCSMObject -Class $Class -filter "Id -eq SR10"
  | Set-SCSMObject -Property Status -Value InProgress
```

Other status values that can be used are `Closed`, `Completed`, `Cancelled`, `Failed`, `Submitted`, `New`, `Active`, `Resolved`, `Pending`, `Editing`.

In Service Manager, we have access management that gives access to various applications, and this can be achieved by implementing different user roles. Application access should be given to a user role and not to specific user accounts. The Service Manager console is capable of assigning and controlling the following user roles for various scenarios.

A user role consists of the following elements (configured when you run the user role wizard):

- User profile
- Queues
- Groups
- Catalog groups

- Tasks
- Views
- Templates
- Users

By selecting specific queues, groups, views, or templates, you can control what a user role will be able to see and do in Service Manager. A user role is a way to assign a user a privileges to perform certain actions in Service Manager. By creating your own objects of the listed types, you are flexible to assign role-based access to the user. The following is the example that illustrates a sample scenario of how we can assign a user role values:

```
$UserRoleArgs = @{
  UserRoleType = "ReadOnlyOperator"
  DisplayName = "restricted role"
  Queue = @()
  Group = @()
  Task = @()
  User = "PSLAB\SCSMUser01"
  }
New-SCSMUserRole @UserRoleArgs
```

The preceding command creates a new read-only operator role, which has access only to forms and views. The PSLAB\SCSMUser01 user has been assigned this user role.

Summary

In this chapter, we covered the fundamentals and got to know how to deal with objects for the automation of the SCSM administration. We also included a few specific cases wherein we covered how to close the incidents and put regulations over it.

We will cover more scenarios specific to the SCSM administration and automation in the next chapter. We will also talk about a few of the real-time examples explaining SCSM capabilities, and that will surely bring more clarity and understanding to the recent chapter.

7
Scenario-based Scripting for SCSM Administration

We now have a basic understanding of how to manage the System Center Service Manager administrative tasks through PowerShell. It's time to look at some of the real-time scenarios that will give you a better understanding of how to use PowerShell to carry out some of the real-life SCSM day-to-day activities. Here, we will cover most of the common scenarios we as administrators perform on a daily basis. We can still do much more than what is covered in this chapter.

This chapter covers the following topics:

- Adding classes to the SCSM allow list
- Exporting management packs
- Backing up unsealed management packs
- Manual activity and service request check
- Tickets status check
- Support group and tier queue check for multiple tickets
- Updating field information for the number of users
- Finding the GUID of any SCSM template
- Getting the queue members for SCSM

 Code blocks demonstrated in this chapter will not include error handling mechanisms. When using the code in real-life scenarios, it is very important to include error handling mechanisms in order to avoid any errors.

For a better understanding of the code blocks used, you can try them in your lab environment and analyze the output. Try to modify the output according to your requirements. This will give you real confidence to write and implement code in the production environment.

Before implementing any code block in production, make sure you have thoroughly tested the code in the development or test environment. Once you have satisfactorily tested the code in the development environment, move the code to the preproduction environment and test its truthiness. Once you are very sure that the script is working perfectly and delivering expected results, implement it in the production environment.

With the assumption that we are clear with the basic exercise that we discussed in the last chapter, we are now good to go with some of the real-time scenarios and the ways to automate them using PowerShell.

Adding classes to the SCSM allow list

This example demonstrates how as an SCSM administrator, we can add classes to the SCSM default allow list. The SCSM allow list is a list of classes to be used by the configuration item Operations Manager 2007 Connector during synchronization. To execute this, we need to import proper management packs to sync data from SCOM to SCSM and also, the object needs to sync to the allow list. Specific to this scenario, at times you might need to add more than one object to the SCSM allow list. Moreover Add-SCSMAllowListClass don't accept input from a pipe line. So, to address this issue, we will get all the class objects required synced with the SCSM allow list in one of the variables, and then pass on the variable to the -ClassName parameter, which in fact accepts array values:

```
$DemoClassNames = Get-SCSMClass | where {$_.Displayname
  -like "*win*"}
```

```
Add-SCSMAllowListClass -ClassName $DemoClassNames
```

The preceding command statements get the result in the $DemoClassNames variable using the Get-SCSMClass cmdlet with the filter provided with it. Once you have the list of the class names in one variable, pass that variable to the -ClassName parameter for the Add-SCSMAllowListClass cmdlet.

Exporting management packs

For those who are new to Sealed and Unsealed management packs, the following is the difference explained in a paragraph taken from

In Service Manager, most of the customization activities are performed using **management packs** (**MP**). Customization activities can be performed for multiple objects, such as notification templates, groups, list items, workflows, and so on. MPs are of two types: Sealed and Unsealed.

A Sealed management pack cannot be modified, but only used as and when required. It has a `.mp` extension. Unsealed management packs are just XML files with the `.xml` extension and can be modified using the SCSM console, or any other method to edit the XML file. A Sealed MP and an Unsealed MP both work best together to achieve most of the scenarios. A Sealed MP has basic functionality added to it, while an Unsealed MP takes care of the customization activities on top of that.

This example will demonstrate how to list and export all the available management packs.

There are a few PowerShell cmdlets available that deal with System Center Service Manager management packs. Before going ahead with the export required management packs, you can use the following methods to import the required SCSM module to avail the supported cmdlets:

1. Open the Windows PowerShell console with the elevated privilege and import the SCSM administration module.

   For SCSM management servers, enter the following line in the console:

   ```
   Import-Module 'C:\Program Files\Microsoft System Center
     2012\Service Manager\Powershell\
     System.Center.Service.Manager.psd1
   ```

2. Open the Service Manager PowerShell console with the elevated privilege. This will indeed import the required module in the background.

   After importing the SCSM module, type the following command statement to export the required management pack.

3. Create a new folder (varies from user to user) `C:\ExportedSCCMMP` to store the exported management packs:

   ```
   Get-SCSMManagementPack | Export-SCSMManagementPack -Path C:\
   ExportedSCCMMP
   ```

4. To export only the Sealed or Unsealed management packs, you can apply a condition using the `Where-Object` statement:

```
Get-SCSMManagementPack | Where-Object {! $_.Sealed} | Export-
SCSMManagementPack -Path C:\ExportedUnsealedSCCMMP
```

```
Get-SCSMManagementPack | Where-Object {$_.Sealed} | Export-
SCSMManagementPack -Path C:\ExportedUnsealedSCCMMP
```

Backing up unsealed management packs

This example will demonstrate how to take a back up of the Unsealed management packs.

As discussed in the previous scenario, there are a few PowerShell cmdlets available that deal with the System Center Service Manager management packs. Before exporting the required management packs, you can use the earlier listed methods to import the required SCSM module.

After importing the SCSM module, type the following command statement to take a back up of the Unsealed management packs:

```
Get-SCSMManagementPack | Where-Object {! $_.Sealed} |
  Export-SCSMManagementPack -Path C:\ExportedUnsealedSCCMMP
```

To export only the Sealed management packs, you can apply a condition using the `Where-Object` statement:

```
Get-SCSMManagementPack | Where-Object {$_.Sealed} |
  Export-SCSMManagementPack -Path C:\ExportedSealedSCCMMP
```

In the preceding example, the command statement will export all the Sealed management packs.

Manual activity and service request check

This example demonstrates how to change the status of a manual activity or service request using PowerShell. The same example can be used to change the status of other activities or requests.

To perform this example, you need to download the external Service Manager module, `SMlets`. We can leverage this module and easily change the status of a ticket for Service Manager. The following are the code statements that can be used to change the status of a manual activity and service request:

```
# Importing module
Import-Module -Name smlets


# Getting details of the manual activity
$ManAct = Get-SCSMObject -Class (Get-SCSMClass -Name
  System.WorkItem.Activity.ManualActivity) -Filter "ID -eq MA1234"


# Changing the status of the manual activity
Set-SCSMObject -SMObject $ManAct -Property Status -Value Completed


# Getting the specific service request
$SerReq = Get-SCSMObject -Class (Get-SCSMClass -Name
  System.WorkItem.ServiceRequest) -filter "ID -eq SR1234"


# Changing the status of the service request to completed
Set-SCSMObject -SMObject $SerReq -Property Status -Value Completed
```

Tickets status check

This example demonstrates how to reopen the tickets if they were closed automatically. We need to supply respective ticket numbers to the `$tid` variable. You can get the ticket ID either from the SCSM console or the respective PowerShell cmdlet:

```
Import-Module SMLets
# Class declaration for Service Request
$Class = Get-SCSMClass -Name System.WorkItem.ServiceRequest
$tid = 'SR123456'
Get-SCSMObject -Class $Class -filter "Id -eq $tid" |
  Set-SCSMObject -Property Status -Value "In Progress"
```

We can use the preceding script block for incidents by replacing the service request declaration with the `$Class = Get-SCSMClass -Name System.WorkItem.Incident` incident declaration.

We just need to provide the respective ID number with the required class declaration based on our environment.

Support group and tier queue check for multiple tickets

The following example will help you modify the support group or tier queue for multiple tickets. Generally, most of us tend to select the wrong support groups and tier queues. It's very important to change the groups to the correct support group and tier queue. For this scenario, we need a list of incidents and service requests in any format of a file that PowerShell can understand and fetch the data from:

```
#Service Request - Correcting Support Group
Import-Module SMLets


# Class declaration for Service Request
$Class = Get-SCSMClass -Name System.WorkItem.ServiceRequest


$TList = Get-Content 'C:\ticket_list.txt'
foreach ($T in $TList)
    {
        Get-SCSMObject -Class $Class -filter "Id -eq $T" |
    Set-SCSMObject -Property SupportGroup -Value "App Catalog"
    }


#Incident - Correcting Tier Queue
Import-Module SMLets


# Class declaration for Incidents
$Class = Get-SCSMClass -Name System.WorkItem.Incident


$TList = Get-Content 'C:\ticket_list.txt'
foreach ($T in $TList)
    {
        Get-SCSMObject -Class $Class -filter "Id -eq $T" |
    Set-SCSMObject -Property TierQueue -Value "App Catalog"
    }
```

Updating field information for a number of users

This example demonstrates how to update the `Employer` field, or any other field, for a large number of users. This can be done manually for a small number of users, but it is very useful if you automate it for a large user base.

In this scenario, we need a user list for the users who want to change or update the field information. A user list can be in any file format that the PowerShell console understands, preferably a text file with one username per line:

```
Import-Module SMLets


# Class declaration for Users
$Class = Get-SCSMClass -Name Microsoft.AD.User


$UList = Get-Content 'C:\users_list.txt'


foreach ($U in $UList)
    {
        Get-SCSMObject -Class $Class -filter "username -eq $U" |
          Set-SCSMObject -Property Company -Value "CompanyName"
        Get-SCSMObject -Class $Class -filter "username -eq $U" |
          Format-Table username, company
    }
```

For each user in the user list, this script block will display the updated information of the company, along with the respective username. For this example, `"CompanyName"` is a hardcoded value for the `Company` property and the user must change it accordingly.

Finding GUID of any SCSM template

This example demonstrates how to find the GUID of any SCSM template. This is a one liner code but very important in certain cases. GUID is a unique value assigned to each SCSM template for better administration:

```
Get-SCSMObjectTemplate | Where-Object {$_.DisplayName -eq
  "Display Name of SCSM Template from Console"} | select Id
```

The preceding command statement will give you an ID that represents the SCSM template uniquely. You can use this information to retrieve or assign this template for further operations.

Getting queue members for SCSM

Many times, we need the information about which objects contain queue members. The following are two ways to find the queue member information using PowerShell:

```
# Using SMLets

$QueueDisplayName = "QueueName"
Import-Module SMLets

# Class declaration for Group
$Class = Get-SCSMClass -Name "System.WorkItemGroup"

$Queue = Get-SCSMObject -Class $Class -Filter
  "DisplayName = '$QueueDisplayName'"

$Relation = Get-SCSMRelationshipClass |
  Where-Object {$_.Source.Class.Name  -eq $Queue.ClassName }

Get-SCSMRelatedObject $Queue -Relationship $Relation

# Using native CMDLETs:
$QueueDisplayName = "QueueName"

Import-Module 'C:\Program Files\Microsoft System Center\
  Service Manager 2012\Powershell\System.Center.Service.Manager.psd1'

$Queue = Get-SCSMQueue -DisplayName $QueueDisplayName
$Relation = Get-SCSMRelationship | Where-Object
  {$_.Source.Type.Id  -eq $Queue.EnterpriseManagementObject.Id }

$Queue.GetRelatedObjectsWhereSource($Relation.Id)
```

The preceding command statement will give you queue members for a given queue and respective relationship.

Summary

In this chapter, you learnt how to use PowerShell to perform various day-to-day activities for Service Manager. This information will give confidence to administrators that use PowerShell to carry out their routine administrative tasks. You saw various scenarios and the usage of PowerShell scripts to get the work done easily without any human error. During the first read the code may look complex, but regular practice can ease the learning.

Going forward, we will see the best practices for all three products covered in this book with relevant scenarios.

8
Best Practices

As we have covered the administration and operation of three System Center products—SCCM, SCOM, and SCSM, we now have full understanding of the PowerShell application of these three products. Let's discuss some real-time applications and derive best practices to use PowerShell with these three products.

This chapter covers the following topics:

- Integrating SQL commands with PowerShell
- SCCM health check activities
- Data warehouse registration

Integrating SQL commands with PowerShell

Since this chapter mainly deals with how to run queries to get results, it is important for us to know the integration of SQL commands with PowerShell. Here is a quick example that demonstrates how to integrate SQL commands with PowerShell.

First, we will see how to create a generic function in PowerShell, which will accept a query as a parameter, execute the query, and return the result. Let's create a generic function by the `Extract-Report` that accepts `$SQLCmd` (which is assumed to be a working SQL query) as a parameter.

Assuming that the `$SQLServer` variable is assigned the SQL server name and `$SQLDatabase` is assigned the SQL instance name, we can use the following function. The function is assuming that the login that is running this PowerShell script has access to the SQL database and uses the Windows authentication method:

```
$global:Log = ".\Log.txt"
Function Extract-Reports([string]$SQLCmd)
```

```
{
    Set-StrictMode -Version Latest
    $authentication = "Integrated Security=SSPI;"

    [Int32]$ConnectionTimeout=15
    [int] $Timeout = 360

    #############################################################
    ## SCCM Site variables
    $connectionString = "Provider=sqloledb; " +
    "Data Source=$SQLserver; " +
    "Initial Catalog=$SQLDatabase; " +
    "$authentication;"

    #############################################################
    ## Making the Connection to the DB
    $connection = New-Object System.Data.OleDb.OleDbConnection
$connectionString
    $connection.Open()
    Add-Content -path $global:Log -Value 'Connected to database'
    foreach($commandString in $SQLCmd)
    {
        $command = New-Object Data.OleDb.OleDbCommand
$commandString,$connection
        $command.CommandTimeout = $timeout

        ## Fetch the results, and close the connection
        $adapter = New-Object System.Data.OleDb.OleDbDataAdapter $command
        $dataset = New-Object System.Data.DataSet
        [void] $adapter.Fill($dataSet)

        ## Return all of the rows from their query
        $dataSet.Tables | Select-Object -Expand Rows
    }
    $connection.Close()
}
```

This function will first establish a connection with the SQL server, execute the command, close the connection with the SQL server, and return the result to the call function.

The next step is to build a sample SQL query and assign the query to the `$SQLCmd` variable. Let's take a simple example that will extract objects from the `PartitionAndGroomingSettings` table:

```
$SQLCmd =@"
SELECT
ObjectName,
GroomingSproc,
DaysToKeep
FROM PartitionAndGroomingSettings WITH (NOLOCK)
"@
```

The next step is to call the function with the SQL command as a parameter:

```
$Result = Extract-Reports $SQLCmd
```

So, now the command will call the function with the SQL query as a parameter and get the results stored in the `$Result` variable.

SCCM health check activities

Being an SCCM administrator, it is very important to have a maintenance task in place to ensure that the environment is always up and running always. There are a few best practices that we follow to ensure the availability of the SCCM server and we call them as health check activities to ensure the availability of the SCCM server.

We can perform the health check activities depending on the environment, activity type, size, and other factors. There are a few tasks that can be performed once a month, a few need to be done weekly, and some daily.

As part of the health check activities, here are the best practices we can follow that can be tested to ensure the availability of the environment:

- Check the SCCM site server availability
- Check the SCCM and dependent service status
- Constantly check the space in the SCCM site server disk
- Constantly check for the SCCM site server memory utilization
- Constantly check for the SCCM site server CPU utilization
- Check for SCCM components availability, such as the management point and distribution point
- Check for the client to management point communication
- Check for any package distribution failures and errors

Let's discuss in detail which tests are required as part of the preceding checks individually and why.

 The $Computer variable in the following examples represents the target computer on which the test will be conducted.

Checking the SCCM site server availability

Here, as part of the SCCM site server availability test, we will perform a simple ping test to ensure that the servers are reachable from the central CAS. We can use the `Test-Connection` cmdlet to check the connectivity status of the site servers:

```
Test-Connection -ComputerName $Computer -Count 2 -Quiet
```

This cmdlet will return either true or false depending on the availability of the site server. If the result is true, we can conclude that the server is reachable at the point in time and if the result is false, the server can be considered to be unreachable.

Checking the SCCM and dependent service status

The services we check as a part of this test depend on the site server roles installed on the server. We are required to test the service status, service startup type, and service state as part of this test. Assuming that the server is loaded with all the roles, we generally check for the following services:

```
SMS_EXECUTIVE
SMS_REPORTING_POINT
SMS_SERVER_LOCATOR_POINT
SMS_SITE_BACKUP
SMS_SITE_COMPONENT_MANAGER
SMS_SITE_VSS_WRITER
SMS_Agent_Host
SMS_System_Health_Validator
```

To test the service status, we can use a simple function that will get the values for each of the services for the specific computer. Depending on the result, we have to conclude the use of the `if` statements whether the service is healthy or unhealthy.

Here is the sample code that demonstrates the service check activities:

```
Function Get-ServiceStatus([string]$Computer, [String]$ServiceName)
{
    $serviceNames = Get-WmiObject Win32_Service -ComputerName $Computer
| where   {$_.Name -eq $ServiceName } | select Name, StartMode, State,
Displayname
    $serviceNames = Get-WmiObject Win32_Service -ComputerName $Computer
| where   {$_.Name -eq $ServiceName } | select Name, StartMode, State,
Displayname
    $serviceNames = Get-WmiObject Win32_Service -ComputerName $Computer
| where   {$_.Name -eq $ServiceName } | select Name, StartMode, State,
DisplayName
    Return $serviceNames
}
```

You can get all these generic functions with different values for the $Computer and $ServiceName variables and compare the value with the standard set. To demonstrate, I will be calling the Get-ServiceStatus function to get the details of the SMS_Agent_Host service running on the CAS.guru.com server:

```
$ServiceStatus = Get-ServiceStatus "CAS.Guru.Com" "SMS_Agent_Host"
# Compare the results with standard configurations
If(($ServiceStatus.State -ne "Running") -or ($ServiceStatus.StartMode
-ne "Auto"))
{
    Write-Host "SMS_Agent_Host on CAS.Guru.Com is running unhealthy"
}
Else
{
    Write-Host "SMS_Agent_Host on CAS.Guru.Com is running healthy"
}
```

Similarly, we can test individually for all the services running across multiple site servers. When we are creating a health check report, instead of writing on a console, we prefer to write a note of the report.

The absence of this service really does not necessarily mean that the site server is unhealthy. We have to check whether the role is installed on the corresponding site server. If the role is not installed, we cannot find the service on the list.

Similarly, we had to check for the existence and status of the dependent services to ensure the functionality of the SCCM environment. The following are the dependent services we mainly look for:

```
IIS Admin Service
WDSSERVER
BITS
Windows Management Instrumentation
```

We can reuse the function to test the service status for the dependent services. Also, we can use similar if-else statements to make a decision on the health of the site server.

 Unlike SCCM services, we have to ensure that the dependent services are present and running on the site servers. We cannot ignore it if the service is not present, as these are basic services (except for the WDS service).

Checking the site server disk space

Here, we check the available free disk space on the site server. We must to ensure that the site server has a good amount of free disk space all the time. Depending on best practices, we can set the threshold on the disk space, after which the server will be considered unhealthy. As a best practice, we can consider the site server with less than 10 GB of disk space unhealthy (the value may be set based on your environment and requirement).

We can use a simple PowerShell code to check the disk space on the site server:

```
$Result = "Healthy"
$disks=Get-WmiObject Win32_Logicaldisk -ComputerName $Computer| Where-
Object {$_.DriveType -eq 3}
foreach($disk in $disks)
{
$freeSpaceGB = [Math]::Round($disk.FreeSpace / 1GB, 2);
If($freeSpaceGB -lt 10)
{
  $Result = "UnHealthy"
}
}
Write-Host "Disk Health = $Result"
```

Site server memory utilization test

We need to consider the memory utilization of the site server as one of the main factors in calling the site server healthy. On the production server, as an administrator, we will be worried if we see the server memory utilization of more than 80 percent. Here is a simple test to check the memory utilization of the site server:

```
$MemoryHealth = "Healthy"
$MemoryStats = Get-WmiObject -Class Win32_OperatingSystem
-ComputerName $Computer| Select-Object TotalVisibleMemorySize,
FreePhysicalMemory

$FreeMemoryinGb = [Math]::Round($MemoryStats.FreePhysicalMemory/ 1MB,
2)
#Note : The unit for the MemoryStats is measured in KB unit.
$UsedMemoryPercentage = 100 - ($MemoryStats.FreePhysicalMemory /
$MemoryStats.TotalVisibleMemorySize * 100)
if($UsedMemoryPercentage -gt 80)
{
   $MemoryHealth = "UnHealthy"
}
Write-Host "Memory Health = $MemoryHealth"
```

Checking for site server CPU utilization

We must always ensure that the CPU utilization of our site server is below 80 percent. Checking CPU utilization is one of our most frequent activities as an SCCM administrator. Here is a simple PowerShell code to check the CPU utilization percentage on the site servers:

```
$CPUHealth = "Healthy"

$CPUUsage = (Get-WmiObject -Class Win32_Processor -ComputerName
$Computer | Select-Object LoadPercentage).LoadPercentage

foreach($CPU in $CPUUsage)
{
  if($CPU -gt 80)
  {
    $CPUHealth = Unhealthy
  }
  else
  {
    $CPUHealth = Healthy
  }
}
Write-Host "CPU Health = $CPUHealth"
```

Checking for SCCM component status

It is very important to ensure the healthy status of all SCCM site components for the proper functionality of the SCCM environment to ensure the healthy status of all SCCM site components. There are many ways in which we can test the Configuration Manager site component's status.

The best way to check the SCCM site component's status is to use the SCCM database and the status messages stored in it. We can look for the entries in the V_SummarizerSiteStatus and v_Site DB view to check the site component's status.

We should ensure that the Status column of the V_Site view should be equal to 1 (which indicates that the component is healthy). We can also see other values, such as 2 for pending installation, 3 for failed, 4 for deleted, and 5 for under upgrade process.

We can use the SQL query integrated with PowerShell to query the SCCM database and get the site component's status.

Checking the management point's health

We can simply use the SCCM database data to ensure the functioning of the management point in the Configuration Manager environment. We can check the v_componentSummarizer view and a different calumet in the table to test the availability of the management point.

The State column in v_componentSummarizer should reflect the value 1 indicating that the component is stated against other values, such as 0 for stopped, 2 for paused, 3 for installing, 4 for reinstalling, and 5 for deinstalling.

Also, the Status column of the v_componentSummarizer view should reflect as 0, indicating that the status is good against other values, such as 1 for warning and 2 for critical.

Apart from the preceding list, we do follow many other health check activities depending on the environment, requirement, need, and work experience of the environment. This is just an outline of how to perform health check activities on the Configuration Manager environment.

SCOM health check report

Like any other tool, it is very important to perform maintenance activities on the SCOM server on a regular basis. There are a few tasks that need daily attention, some need weekly, and a few monthly. As an Operations Manager administrator, we have to decide how frequently the task needs attention.

There are a few maintenance tasks that we perform on the SCOM server on a regular basis to ensure the functionality of the monitoring environment. These include:

- Checking the disk space of the operation database and data warehouse
- Checking for the fast growing tables in the operation database and data warehouse
- Listing top event-generating computers
- Top alert-by-alert count
- Database grooming history
- Maintenance mode report
- Management pack and overrides modification details

The list goes on depending on your environment and requirements. The main idea here is to give a basic introduction to health check operations that we can perform on the SCOM server. Here are a few hints on how to perform some of the listed critical individual activities.

Checking disk space of operation database and data warehouse

To ensure the availability and performance of Operations Manager, it is very important to keep an eye on the operation database and data warehouse. We can check the size of the database by querying the sysfiles table of the database. We can also keep monitoring the TempBD size using the same table.

Though SQL installation for operation database and data warehouse is a one-time activity, it is important to retrieve the version details of SQL in the health check report. This gives a clear idea of the environment infrastructure to the management. We can use the following query to get the version details from the SQL server:

```
SELECT SERVERPROPERTY('productversion') AS "Product Version",
SERVERPROPERTY('productlevel') AS "Service Pack", SERVERPROPERTY
('edition') AS "Edition"
```

Querying top-event and alert-generating computers

It is important to note the top event-generating computers. This helps us to analyze problems with the environment and sometimes they are also required to fine tune the management packs accordingly (maybe rectifying the false alerts, suppressing repeated alerts, and so on).

We can use a simple SQL query to get the list of, say, the top-20 event-generating computers. We can get the details by querying the `EventAllView` table to log the computer name columns:

```
SELECT top 20 LoggingComputer, COUNT(*) AS TotalEvents
FROM EventallView
GROUP BY LoggingComputer
ORDER BY TotalEvents DESC
```

Also, we can get a list of the computer-generated top alert count by number using an SQL query. We can get this count by querying `AlertView` using the following query:

```
SELECT Top 20 AlertStringName, Name, SUM(1) AS
SumCount, SUM(RepeatCount+1) AS AlertCount
FROM AlertView WITH (NOLOCK)
GROUP BY AlertStringName, Name
ORDER BY AlertCount DESC
```

Data grooming settings

It is very important to track the configured data grooming settings configured to ensure the proper maintenance of the Operations Manager environment. We can track the grooming settings by querying the `PartitionAndGroomingSettings` table from the database:

```
SELECT ObjectName, GroomingSproc, DaysToKeep, GroomingRunTime,DataGroo
medMaxTime FROM PartitionAndGroomingSettings
```

Reporting all objects in the maintenance mode

As an SCOM administrator, it is important to keep track of SCOM objects in maintenance mode. We can get the details by querying the `MaintenanceMode` table to get the object details. To get the human-readable display name, we combine the table with the `BaseManagedEntityId` table:

```
SELECT DisplayName, ResonCode, Comments from dbo.MaintenanceMode mm
JOIN dbo.BaseManagedEntity bm on mm.BaseManagedEntityId =
bm.BaseManagedEntityId
WHERE Path is NULL and IsInMaintenanceMode = 1
```

Changing the SCSM subscription property by PowerShell

Being an SCSM administrator, sometimes you might need to change the subscription details of Service Manager. It is important for administrators to do this activity without any error, as it is directly propositional to all other SCSM activities. We can use the following code block to achieve this:

```
$SCSMSubName = Get-SCSMSubscription -ComputerName SCSM001 | where {$_.
DisplayName -eq "Name of SCSM subscription"}"}"}

$SCSMSubName.Description = "This is SCSM description"

Update-SCSMSubscription -Description $SCSMSubName
```

Data warehouse registration

While using Service Manager for data warehouse servers, the first and most important thing that we perform is we register the data warehouse source. Data warehouse registration has nothing to do with administrative functions, but this is the essential step to perform reporting to functions for certain activities. This step will link the Service Manager management group to the data warehouse management group. We can use the following code block to register the data warehouse source:

```
# Importing required module
Import-Module "C:\Program Files\Microsoft System Center 2012\Service
Manager\Microsoft.EnterpriseManagement.Warehouse.Cmdlets.dll"
# Getting proper credentials
$DWCred = Get-Credential
```

```
# Registering Source for Data Warehouse server
Register-SCDWSource -DataSourceTypeName ServiceManager
-SourceComputerName SCSDW001 -SourceCredential $DWCred
```

 Please provide `SourceComputerName` as your data warehouse server.

To unregister the data warehouse source at any point of time, use the following command statement with proper parameter values:

```
# Unregistering Source for Data Warehouse server
Unregister-SCDWSource -DataSourceTypeName ServiceManager -
DataSourceName "SCSDW001"
```

Summary

With this chapter we are declaring the end of our book. We covered best practices and scenarios in this particular section with respect to all the three products. In the earlier chapters, we covered many examples and scenarios with the basic and intermediate knowledge of these products: SCSM, SCOM, and SCSM.

Hope you have a better life with System Center products, along with the proper PowerShell automation in place. As always, *sharing is caring!*

Index

Symbols

.csv/.txt file input
  multiple packages, creating 43

A

administration, SCOM
  about 58
  agent management 58, 59
  management packs 61, 62
  management server 58
administrative cmdlets 83
agent management
  about 58, 59
  agent installation 59, 60
  SCOM proxy agents 60, 61
aggregate monitor 65
alert management 54
alert notifications 67, 68
alert resolution 55
application catalog web service point
  creating 34, 35
application catalog website point roles
  creating 34, 35
asset and compliance
  alert management 28
  client settings information, obtaining 27, 28
  collection details, obtaining 21-23
  Configuration Manager objects,
      handling 26
  Configuration Manager status
      messages, reading 23
  information, gathering 21
  new user/device collections, creating 23-25

authoring, SCOM
  about 56
  class 57
  discovery management 56
  groups 57
  instance 57

B

boot images 36, 37

C

central administrative site (CAS) 49
class, SCOM 57
cmdlets, Service Manager
  administrative cmdlets 83
  data warehouse cmdlets 83
Common Engineering Criteria (CEC) 3
Configuration Manager
  alert management 28
  boundary details, obtaining 16, 17
  component status, obtaining 50, 51
  discovery details, obtaining 16
  distribution points details, obtaining 18, 20
  hierarchy details 15
  installation directory getting,
      PowerShell used 44
  management point details, obtaining 20
  new user/device collections, creating 23-25
  objects, handling 26
  other site role details, obtaining 21
  site details, obtaining 15
  status messages, reading 23
  using 14

Configuration Manager environment
list of all site servers, obtaining 49
list of primary sites, obtaining 49

D

database grooming 67
data warehouse
registration 113, 114
cmdlets 83
dependency monitor 65
Desired State Configuration (DSC) 3
discovery management 56
distribution point group (DP group) 42

G

**Get-CMSoftwareUpdateAutoDeployment
Rule cmdlet 40**
Get-CMSoftwareupdate cmdlet 39
**Get-CMSoftwareUpdateDeployment
Package cmdlet 40**
Get-CMSoftwareUpdateGroup cmdlet 39
gray agents, SCOM
exporting 74
listing 74
groups, SCOM 57
GUID
about 99
searching 99

H

health check activities, SCCM
alert-generating computers, querying 112
component status, checking 110
CPU utilization, checking 109
data grooming settings, tracking 112
data warehouse, disk space checking 111
dependent service status, checking 106, 107
maintenance tasks, performing 111
management point health, checking 110
objects, reporting in maintenance mode 113
operation database, disk
space checking 111
performing 105
SCCM site server availability, checking 106
site server disk space, checking 108

site server memory utilization,
checking 109
subscription property, changing by
PowerShell 113
top-event generating computers,
querying 112
heartbeat failure machines
listing 79

I

IIS 7 application
putting, in maintenance mode 81
incident reporting 87, 88
**Information Technology Infrastructure
Library (ITIL) 83**
installation
SCCM client agent version 51
instance, SCOM 57

M

management group 54
management packs (MP), SCOM
about 61, 62, 95
alert notifications 67, 68
database grooming 67
reference link 76
SCOM monitors 65, 66
SCOM rules 63-65
management servers
health status, listing 80
listing, in maintenance mode 80
Microsoft .Net Framework 4.0
URL 5
Microsoft Operations Framework (MOF) 83
monitoring, SCOM
alert filtering 53
alert management 53, 54
alert resolution 53, 55
management group 54
multiple distribution points
adding, to distribution point group 42
assumption 43
prescripting activities 42
multiple packages
creating, with .csv/.txt file input 43
prescripting activities 44

Thank you for buying
Microsoft System Center PowerShell Essentials

About Packt Publishing

Packt, pronounced 'packed', published its first book, *Mastering phpMyAdmin for Effective MySQL Management*, in April 2004, and subsequently continued to specialize in publishing highly focused books on specific technologies and solutions.

Our books and publications share the experiences of your fellow IT professionals in adapting and customizing today's systems, applications, and frameworks. Our solution-based books give you the knowledge and power to customize the software and technologies you're using to get the job done. Packt books are more specific and less general than the IT books you have seen in the past. Our unique business model allows us to bring you more focused information, giving you more of what you need to know, and less of what you don't.

Packt is a modern yet unique publishing company that focuses on producing quality, cutting-edge books for communities of developers, administrators, and newbies alike. For more information, please visit our website at www.packtpub.com.

About Packt Enterprise

In 2010, Packt launched two new brands, Packt Enterprise and Packt Open Source, in order to continue its focus on specialization. This book is part of the Packt Enterprise brand, home to books published on enterprise software – software created by major vendors, including (but not limited to) IBM, Microsoft, and Oracle, often for use in other corporations. Its titles will offer information relevant to a range of users of this software, including administrators, developers, architects, and end users.

Writing for Packt

We welcome all inquiries from people who are interested in authoring. Book proposals should be sent to author@packtpub.com. If your book idea is still at an early stage and you would like to discuss it first before writing a formal book proposal, then please contact us; one of our commissioning editors will get in touch with you.

We're not just looking for published authors; if you have strong technical skills but no writing experience, our experienced editors can help you develop a writing career, or simply get some additional reward for your expertise.

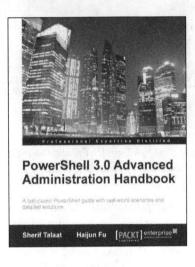

**PowerShell 3.0 Advanced
Administration Handbook**

ISBN: 978-1-84968-642-6   Paperback: 370 pages

A fast-paced PowerShell guide with real-world
scenarios and detailed solutions

1. Discover and understand the concept of
    Windows PowerShell 3.0.

2. Learn the advanced topics and techniques for a
    professional PowerShell scripting.

3. Explore the secret of building custom
    PowerShell snap-ins and modules.

4. Take advantage of PowerShell integration
    capabilities with other technologies for better
    administration skills.

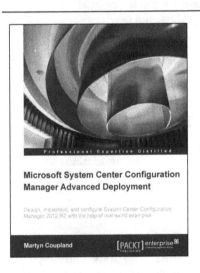

**Microsoft System Center
Configuration Manager Advanced
Deployment**

ISBN: 978-1-78217-208-6   Paperback: 290 pages

Design, implement, and configure System Center
Configuration Manager 2012 R2 with the help of
real-world examples

1. Learn how to design and operate Configuration
    Manager 2012 R2 sites.

2. Explore the power of Configuration
    Manager 2012 R2 for managing your
    client and server estate.

3. Discover up-to-date solutions to real-world
    problems in System Center Configuration
    Manager administration.

Please check **www.PacktPub.com** for information on our titles

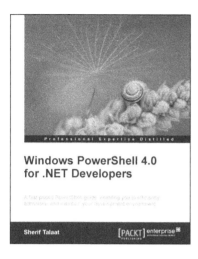

Windows PowerShell 4.0 for .NET Developers

ISBN: 978-1-84968-876-5   Paperback: 140 pages

A fast-placed PowerShell guide, enabling you to efficiently administer and maintain your development environment

1. Enables developers to start adopting Windows PowerShell in their own application to extend its capabilities and manageability.

2. Introduces beginners to the basics, progressing on to advanced level topics and techniques for professional PowerShell scripting and programming.

3. Step-by-step guide, packed with real world scripts examples, screenshots, and best practices.

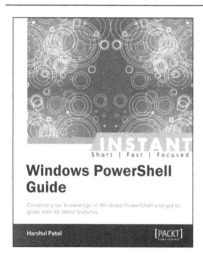

Instant Windows PowerShell Guide

ISBN: 978-1-84968-678-5   Paperback: 86 pages

Enhance your knowledge of Windows PowerShell and get to grips with its latest features

1. Learn something new in an Instant! A short, fast, focused guide delivering immediate results.

2. Understand new CMDLETs and parameters with relevant examples.

3. Discover new module functionality such as CIM, Workflow, DSC, and so on.

Please check **www.PacktPub.com** for information on our titles

9781784397142